# DIVING TO ADVENTURE!

## How To Get the Most Fun From Your Diving & Snorkeling

## by  M. Timothy O'Keefe

### The Diving Series

A LARSEN'S OUTDOOR PUBLISHING BOOK
THE ROWMAN & LITTLEFIELD PUBLISHING GROUP, INC.
Lanham • Chicago • New York • Toronto • Plymouth, UK

Published by
LARSEN'S OUTDOOR PUBLISHING
An imprint of The Rowman & Littlefield Publishing Group, Inc.
4501 Forbes Boulevard, Suite 200, Lanham, Maryland 20706
http://www.rlpgtrade.com

Estover Road, Plymouth PL6 7PY, United Kingdom

Distributed by National Book Network

British Library Cataloguing in Publication Information Available

**Library of Congress Cataloging-in-Publication Data Available**

Library of Congress 92-74327

ISBN: 978-0-936513-30-0 (paper: alk.paper)

☉™ The paper used in this publication meets the minimum
requirements of American National Standard for Information
Sciences—Permanence of Paper for Printed Library Materials,
ANSI/NISO Z39.48-1992.

Printed in the United States of America

# DEDICATION

This work is dedicated to Cap'n Don Stewart, dive pioneer extraordinaire, Bonaire, Netherlands Antilles. Thanks, Uncle Don, for always keeping the fun in diving.

# ABOUT THE AUTHOR

M. Timothy O'Keefe has been a diver for more than 30 years. His articles and photographs have appeared in numerous publications worldwide, including National Geographic Society books; Time-Life Books; Rodale's Scuba Diving, SCUBA Times, Diving & Snorkeling, Caribbean Travel & Life, Newsweek, Travel & Leisure and more.

With Larry Larsen, he was co-author of "Fish & Dive the Caribbean, Vol. 1" which was a finalist in the annual competition of the National Association of Independent Publishers. Chosen from 500 other entries for Best Content, the judges said: "An excellent source book with invaluable instructions for fishing or diving. Written by two nationally-known experts who, indeed, know what vacationing can be!"

Tim holds a PhD from the University of North Carolina at Chapel Hill and is a professor in the School of Communication at the University of Central Florida in Orlando, where he established the journalism program. He is a member of the Outdoor Writers Association of America (OWAA), the Society of American Travel Writers (SATW) and a past president of the Florida Outdoor Writers Association (FOWA).

# PREFACE

All of us remember books or movies that had a formative impact on our lives. For me, it was a book I devoured at least once a year in junior high and high school. It was by the man who will, for my generation, be the true father of sport diving: Dr. Hans Hass of Austria. Hass accomplished many firsts: developing the first underwater camera, being the first to photograph sharks in their natural habitat, and producing feature-length documentaries that were shown around the world. It could not have been easy: Hass began his pioneer diving with only a mask and fins--no snorkel. The aqua-lung had yet to be invented.

I still marvel that his complete translated works were available at Douglas S. Freeman, a brand new high school located in land-locked Richmond, VA. I wish now I had met the librarian responsible for acquiring those books. He or she was as much a dreamer as I; and I have been fortunate enough to live out many of those dreams.

Including the chance to dive with my boyhood hero. I met Hans Hass on the island of Bonaire in the Netherlands Antilles, the primary location of his first encounters with marine life. It was an unforgettable week diving with Hass and his wife Lottie.

Yet now Hans Hass, the very first to promote and publicize the sport, is all but forgotten in the U.S. except by us old-timers. By the end of the 40s, Hans Hass had accomplished what he needed to underwater, and he went on to other things. Since the 1950s, he has been eclipsed by the feats of Jacques Cousteau, co-inventor of the aqua-lung, which opened the subsea world to everyone. Cousteau's TV specials during the 1970s, 80s and 90s probably did more to promote interest in diving and appreciation of the marine environment than anything else.

But for me, Hass will always be the true pioneer of sport diving. Without his books as a constant source of inspiration in high school, my life would have been so different; so much more bland. It is because of my special affection for Hass and his contributions that this present book's title is adapted from his very first work. Some might consider this the height of presumption, but I believe he would understand and, I think, appreciate it.

Unlike Hass' book, this is not an account of my adventures. Instead, it is a road map for discovering your own.

Good hunting.

# CONTENTS

Dedication ................................................................................3
About The Author .................................................................3
Preface ....................................................................................5
Introduction - Diving To Adventure ................................9
1. Cozying Up To Sea Critters ............................... 13
2. Creature Feature - The Sea Horse ..................... 21
3. Beginning Underwater Photography ................. 27
4. Easy Macro Photography .................................... 37
5. Collecting And Preserving Artifacts ................. 43
6. Thrill Of Night Diving ....................................... 51
7. Stalking The Wily Lobster ................................. 59
8. Using Current To Your Advantage ................... 67
9. Wintertime Pool Games ..................................... 75
10. Coping With Seasickness .................................... 85
11. Does Diving Hurt Your Hearing? ..................... 91
12. Planning A Dive Vacation .................................. 97
13. The ABC's Of Live-Aboard Dive Vacations ...... 107
14. The World's Ten Best Scuba Vacations ............. 117
15. The World's Ten Best Snorkeling Sites ............. 129
16. Travel Tips For The Tropics ............................... 141
Resource Directory ............................................................ 149
Index ................................................................................ 158

# DIVING TO ADVENTURE

## Introduction

You and I are among the most fortunate people ever to live. We are the first in the earth's history able to visit and breathe underwater, an environment as foreign to mankind as space.

You and I are more fortunate than the astronauts. In the undersea world, we are guaranteed to encounter bizarre sights and strange creatures far more interesting than anything space travelers have yet witnessed. Space, after all, is a void, a great emptiness.

The undersea world, on the other hand, teems with life. Thanks to the invention of scuba, you and I are the first to have the opportunity to visit an alien--though not essentially hostile--world where our present state-of-the-art equipment still limits us as only temporary visitors.

Yet again, we surpass the astronauts. We divers get to tangibly experience our watery environment and not be isolated from it by the bulk of a life support suit. On the other hand, a walk in space is still an extraordinary event.

Considering our good fortune to be born at this historic time, I have always been astounded at diving's tremendous drop-out rate. It is one of the highest of any sport. Within two years of training, the majority of certified divers stop diving. Why?

It's certainly not because of physical limitations. You and I can dive for the rest of our lives if we remain in reasonable health. That's an advantage not possible in many sports: when the knees, elbows and stamina wear out, the playing days are over. The super jocks of one era are the couch potatoes of the next.

*Divers and astronauts both visit alien environments. Diving, however, is within the means of anyone.*

Not so for us divers and snorkelers. We can go on forever. Look at Cousteau. Look at yourself.

What does it take to be a diver? Nothing, but getting in the water. And, like anything else, to enjoy what you're doing.

The long-time divers I know develop beyond just sightseers. They become photographers. They collect artifacts. They hunt for treasure. They attempt challenging activities, such as night diving (an incredibly renewing experience), or they travel to far off places around the world, to sightsee or photograph.

There is no reason to ever become bored diving. If it happens, something's wrong. Diving doesn't change, but perhaps our appreciation of it does.

It's like getting our first driver's license. Just being able to drive is a remarkable feat at first. Then it becomes commonplace. But we certainly don't give up driving, because it allows us to achieve important things we couldn't otherwise.

That initial ability to dive or snorkel is even more remarkable. But I suspect that unless we use diving as we do an automobile--as a means to accomplish something--diving and snorkeling also turn routine.

I began scuba diving at the age of 13, more than 30 years ago, before there were certifying agencies. My own interest has ebbed at times, usually when there were pressing events occurring in my land-based life: college and graduate school, marriage, birth of a son, divorce.

But once underwater cameras and strobes achieved a certain level of sophistication in the 1970s, I was hooked for good. The purpose of this book is to keep you just as hooked on diving. By traveling extensively around the world, I've been fortunate enough to experience sport diving in a way few people have.

Drawing on more than three decades of experience (a time frame more alarming than impressive) I've attempted to describe in some depth a variety of activities that should keep anyone hooked on diving: what to do, where to go.

I'm interested in your reaction. What did you find most interesting or helpful? What was left out? Please write to me at Larsen's Outdoor Publishing and let me know.

Diving is today's only true pioneering sport: mankind has batted around balls and slid down mountains for centuries. How can anyone not appreciate this unique opportunity?

If tickets were sold for the space shuttle, people would line up for them. Diving is equally challenging, far less costly, and certainly safer.

M. Timothy O'Keefe
Longwood, FL

# Chapter 1

## COZYING UP TO SEA CRITTERS

### Getting Acquainted Underwater

Fish. Starfish. Shrimp. Sponges. Although the names of these creatures are familiar to everyone, it doesn't take divers and snorkelers long to learn how startling different these animals can be in their different shapes and colors. They make aliens created for science fiction movies seem drab in comparison.

As a result, even people who disliked science class in school usually find themselves turning part naturalist once they take up snorkeling or scuba. As famed explorer Jacques Cousteau noted, "The creatures of the undersea world, seemingly infinite in their number and form, can only amaze a diver when he first sees them. In a way, it is like a return to the myths and creatures of one's childhood, which were also populated with unique and bizarre beings. Only underwater, these fabulous creatures are for real."

Furthermore, marine animals are a lot more agreeable about being observed than wild animals on land. Fish and other creatures may hide at the first approach of a diver, but then they reappear to go about their business, though still keeping a wary, watchful eye on the large object that's just entered their domain.

Land animals, on the other hand, usually flee at the first whiff or sight of man, never to be spotted again. Wildlife viewing is far easier underwater, and it's not uncommon to encounter scores of wild animals on just a single one-hour dive. Land naturalists can't often make the same claim.

Regardless of whether you're in fresh or salt water, the first thing you're likely to notice are the fish. Species that can be so elusive in taking a baited hook will sometimes be more than happy to take food from a diver's hand. Unless they've encountered spearfishermen, most fresh and salt water species are curious about divers and will often come within arm's reach.

Unfortunately, fish are not plentiful everywhere. Fresh water fish such as bass and bream tend to be found near vegetation or some sort of structure, such as logs or sunken debris. Most fresh water fish appear to be the same color, a kind or dirty green or brown. This is because the full properties of light do not penetrate very deep into the water, and so the full spectrum of color isn't available. However, if you shine a light or use a strobe for your pictures, the full bright colors you're accustomed to will suddenly appear.

Compared to salt water species, the variety of fish in fresh water is more limited and their smaller size may make them less impressive. Still, as one diver notes, "There's just something about seeing any fish underwater that makes it interesting. You even find yourself going out of the way to see a carp or catfish or a gar, things you wouldn't even want to look at if you were an angler."

While there is more than enough to keep any fresh water diver occupied, ocean divers almost always enjoy better wildlife viewing. Fish watching is so popular that waterproof field guides are available for you to take into the ocean guides so you can keep track of the numerous species.

Of course, you don't need a guide book to spot sharks and barracudas, both of which cause some discomfort among new divers the first time they encounter them. Yet, except for the great white sharks frequently found off Australia, most sharks rarely trouble divers.

*Divers do sometimes willingly mix with sharks. These divers are feeding small blacktip sharks in the Bahamas.*

Dr. Hans Hass of Austria, the first man ever to film sharks underwater, says "Sharks are shy, very shy. Anytime they see a diver in the water they could attack--so why don't they? The answer is they are attuned to certain patterns that signify prey for them, and the human doesn't fit into this pattern, except perhaps for the white shark and the deep-sea sharks that are so big they consider any object in the sea as potential food."

Despite all the lurid tales, shark attacks are rare. Accident statistics show that more people die from bee stings or lightning strikes than are attacked by sharks. Considering the millions of people who go into the water every year, those are excellent odds. And as divers like to point out, it is usually swimmers and surfers--not divers or snorkelers--who are bitten.

Sharks do not often frequent the same waters popular with divers, but the same cannot be said for the barracuda...which is perhaps even more harmless. While sharks look graceful and have the decency to swim with their mouths closed, barracuda always look mean and don't attempt to hide their sharp dentures. Their famous 'cuda yawn,' where they open their mouths wide for no apparent reason except to scare everyone, is unnerving the first time you see it.

Barracuda also have an annoying habit of escorting divers, always staying well out of reach but still close enough to make new divers nervous. Swimming with barracudas is a fact of life in many warm waters, and people usually adjust to it very quickly. Barracuda attacks are even rarer than shark bites. When they occur, it's normally because a diver was wearing a flashing bracelet and the cuda made a grab for it, just as it would for a reflecting fishing lure.

Actually, the creatures that are responsible for most injuries in salt water aren't even fish at all. They are the sea urchins, the mobile pin cushions that populate the ocean floor and coral reefs. Fortunately, sea urchins never deliberately attack, as porcupines reportedly do. Instead, careless divers sometimes walk--and yes, even sit--on them instead of paying attention to what they're doing. The spines are not poisonous, just painful. If a spine happens to break off in the skin, it will usually work itself out in a day or two, just like a splinter.

Recognizing that sharks, barracudas and sea urchins are only potential problems--just as an automobile can be--there's really little to worry about in terms of the marine life. Instead, as professional dive organizations have pointed out for years, the riskiest part of diving takes place before and after the dive: the drive to and from the swim site.

On all sea coasts the varieties of fish you'll see can be astounding. Among the most common are the prison-striped sargeant majors, the buck-toothed parrot fish, the stately-looking angels and thick-lipped, big-mouth grouper.

*It's happening more and more often: divers encountering wild dolphin in the open ocean who want to play.*

On rare occasions you may even spot a dolphin, but usually these animals are too shy to venture close to divers. Plus, there are the jacks, snapper--the list is incredible. Even the most complete fish guide doesn't contain all the varieties you're likely to see in some places.

Many smaller salt water species go under the general name 'reef fish' or 'tropicals' because they are normally found around coral reefs. Corals, another group of animals entirely, combine to form the hard, massive reef structures that captains of Spanish treasure galleons discovered slice through their boat hull as easily as a knife passes through mustard. Scientists say that the part of the coral reef divers see is actually the skeleton of countless small coral animals, known as polyps, which normally hide inside their protective limestone covering. Despite the size of their works, polyps are quite small, only about 1/10 to 1/2 inch in length. Naturalists consider a coral reef to be a gigantic graveyard of sorts, since for a reef to form, many animals must die. It is only the outer layer of a reef that is alive. The main bulk is composed of dead skeletons which support the living corals. When a coral dies, its spot is soon taken over and built upon by another coral, usually of the same species.

Coral colonies often assume intricate, elaborate shapes. And it is startling how similar in form some corals are to the shapes found on land. The massive stands of elkhorn and staghorn corals richly deserve their names. It's as though some sculptor, finding the shapes once pleasing, sought to duplicate them in a totally different environment.

Scientists claim there are more than 200 different types of corals in the Atlantic, Pacific and Caribbean. Some grow in huge mounds, like boulders. Others resemble trees and shrubs, delicate lace-work formations, so fragile-looking that the slightest wave action should rip them apart; yet they are as hard as concrete.

The small coral polyps themselves, master builders of these huge reef networks, are hardly as imposing looking. In general, their bodies are sac-like, and they have a mouth surrounded by a ring or several rings of tentacles. These wavy tentacles, used to paralyze and kill small prey by sending out small stinging threads, once made scientists believe corals were plants instead of animals. Most coral stings are too weak to be felt by humans. However, every diver will testify that the so-called fire coral gained its name properly. The mustard-colored coral has a thin white edge, and just the slightest contact results in pain. Ammonia and meat tenderizer help reduce the pain.

Although the reefs themselves are quite hard, they are encased by a soft, greasy-feeling tissue. If this tissue is damaged by touching and scraping, it's possible the entire

*A snorkeler swims over a bed of eel grass thickly populated with short-spined sea urchins.*

coral colony will be affected by disease or infection. Understandably, most dive operators want divers to stay off the coral and not to wear gloves. Without gloves, divers are less likely to grab hold of the reef.

Some corals in the Atlantic and Caribbean are soft and limber. Technically, these are known as octocorals since each of the polyps has eight tentacles; hard corals often have many more. Although sometimes referred to as soft corals, these are a different category of the true soft corals of the Pacific.

Numerous other creatures besides fish live on and around coral reefs. Many actually live on the reef itself or inside its crevices, making the reef a vast condominium. The actual number of these creatures is unknown; new ones are being discovered almost annually.

Some, like the sponges, have names that are familiar. Yet most sponges look nothing like the utensils used for washing cars and dishes. Live ocean sponges come in enough colors to match every shade of lipstick ever invented and probably a few that haven't. They bear little resemblance to the flat, squared sponges sold in stores.

Instead, they come in the shape of barrels big enough for a person to sit inside. Others are tall and tube-like. The encrusting sponges which grow on docks and piers are thin and elongated like roof shingles, while the golf ball sponges match their name in both shape and size.

Colorful and distinctive as the sponges are, many divers find the bizarre-looking nudibranchs more interesting. Nudibranchs are mollusks that have no shell. They sometimes look like small snails with a sharply defined but harmless set of horns. Their colors can be wild and garish, as if someone accidentally mixed together several kinds of paint.

Ribbon nudibranchs look like ridged pieces of lasagna noodles stacked in layers. Their colors often seem softer than the last rays of a sunset.

Shrimp, too, come in many sizes and colors. The mantis shrimp has arms like that of the land mantis, but it is far bigger and much more impressive looking. And the banded coral shrimp in its elaborate red and white stripes looks more like a piece of jewelry than something you'd find on the ocean floor.

Crabs, octopus, worms, manta rays--the list of animals you may encounter goes on and on, seemingly limitless. As one diver describes it, "With always something new to discover, it is like being a kid again and finding a fantastic Christmas parade that never ends."

# Chapter 2

## CREATURE FEATURE - THE SEA HORSE

### Legendary Steed of the Gods

For many years, the sea horse was considered only a legendary creature, no more to be believed in than the unicorn or the winged Pegasus of ancient mythology.

It was the sea horse that served as the steed of the Greek gods, the power that pulled Neptune's wedding chariot. Later, the sea horse became the symbol of nobility in Medieval heraldry for those who distinguished themselves at sea. With such a background, understandably the sea horse was considered too fantastic a creature to be real.

Today, sea horses are a favorite subject of underwater photographers and the most sought-after object on many Caribbean dives. Yet it is hard to shake off childish memories when you encounter your first sea horse, whether in the ocean or at an aquarium. There is so much mystery that surrounds these gentle animals.

It's only natural that a creature so shrouded in fable should also be believed to have magical powers. For instance, a sea horse mixed with other liquids was once supposed to cure baldness, cancer and even the bite of a mad dog. For all the good it could do, the sea horse also was the main ingredient of many Medieval poisons. And today in the Orient, sea horses are sold as an aphrodisiac.

Few other animals have been credited with the power to accomplish so much.

It usually comes as a surprise to new divers to learn that the sea horse is actually a fish since it certainly doesn't resemble one and it swims vertically, powered by small dorsal and pectoral fins, another unusual characteristic for a fish.

The sea horse also lacks the speed characteristic of a fish. Instead, it moves slowly, although its fins beat at a fantastic rate, moving back and forth as much as 35 times per second. Better harnessed, this power obviously would be incredible.

The sea horse has also been called a living elevator, since when it wishes to ascend or descend it normally does so vertically. To ascend, it uncurls its tail; to descend, it curls up its tail and arches its neck and seems literally to fall.

Despite its small size (generally two to six inches) and slow speed, the sea horse is as heavily armored as a tank. Its outer skeleton of interlocking bony plates shine like a newly waxed car, which makes them look more like plastic toys than living animals. At the points where the plates come together, they join small knobs and waffle-shaped spines, as many as 60 on some species. The sea horse also has an internal skeleton, but it lacks one normal feature: there are no ribs.

Another peculiar feature of the sea horse is the fact it has a neck, again something lacking on most fish. And, too, there is the shape of its head. Except for the fact its mouth is tube-shaped, the head truly does resemble that of a horse.

The manner in which a sea horse eats is as remarkable as its appearance. It has no teeth but relies on sucking in its food with its tube-shaped mouth. The method, however, is so effective it pulls in small shrimp and other minute animals at bullet-like speed.

Once a sea horse has captured its food, it carries out its digestion just as unconventionally. It has no stomach, so it has to rely on food absorption through its simply organized intestinal system. Scientists are not sure whether this stomachless condition is the result of retarded evolution or incomplete development, where the animal remains in the larval stage

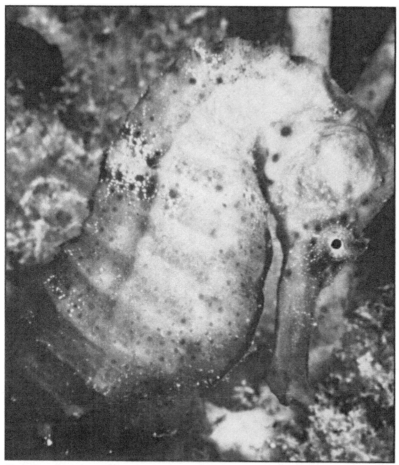

*Sea horses usually are most visible at night. They will often masquerade with a color akin to whatever they happen to be holding onto with their tail.*

even though it achieves sexual maturity. It is yet another mystery of the sea horse.

If the sea horse did not have such a distinctive shape, it is possible it would have received the name sea chameleon, so good is it at changing its color and camouflage. This ability undoubtedly has been of paramount importance in the sea horses's survival. Such a small, slow moving creature otherwise might have departed us a long time ago.

Very often a sea horse will masquerade with a color akin to whatever it happens to be holding onto with its tail, seeming to become just another projection of whatever object it's attached itself to. This, both in the wild and in aquariums, is how the sea horse is normally seen, standing upright with its tail anchoring it in place.

Sea horses use an odd method to rear their young. If, as some say, the sea horse invented the concept of women's lib, it certainly has refined it to the extreme. There are not many species where after a few conjugal moments the male gets stuck with raising the offspring while the female goes off to find a new mate to horse around with.

The courtship process can be initiated by either males or females. It begins by the animals intertwining tails. Then one partner begins gyrating from one end to the other. Once the animal who started this ritual finishes, the other begins. A pair may take turns for as long as 20-30 minutes.

Then they embrace. It's at this time the female deposits her eggs in the male's brood pouch, filling it with as many eggs as it will hold. Then she is off, perhaps to begin another courtship. However, if she has failed to fill the male's pouch, he will seek out other females to accommodate him.

Once the male's pouch is full, it essentially turns into a placenta, allowing the now pregnant male, looking awkward and ungainly, to supply nutrients and oxygen and dispose of waste products until the young are born 30-50 days later. As many as 250-600 eggs may be carried by a male at one time, depending on his size.

When it's time for the youngsters to be on their own, the male expels them from his pouch through a series of muscular contractions not unlike those of a woman.

The baby sea horses are expelled over a series of days, anywhere from 10 to 30 pushed out at a time. Once they all are out, the male's brood pouch becomes shapeless again, and shortly thereafter he is able to be saddled again with another round of child support if he so desires.

Once out in the open sea, the young sea horses (like their parents) become possible appetizers for any number of spe-

*A seahorse may be only the size of your little finger. Search carefully.*

cies. Skates, rays, sharks and many fish dine on sea horses. Sea horses may look strange, but apparently they taste pretty good.

In recent years, there's been considerable interest in raising sea horses in home aquariums. Because they are a salt water species, the sea horse is much more difficult to maintain than so-called "tropical" fresh water fish. The sea horse must remain in an ocean-type environment or it will die.

Marine aquariums require constant care and should not be attempted unless you can check on changes in salinity and other elements frequently. Sea horse stables (as such aquariums are called) normally have both charcoal and bottom filters to remove contaminants.

With proper care and attention, sea horses can thrive in such environments for years. But the experts advise that raising sea horses should not be attempted on a casual basis, that this will only end up destroying them.

In many ways, the sea horse seems like it was put together from left-over parts of other animals and assembled in such haste that a few of the more common components (ribs, stomach and teeth) were left out. In her excellent book "Encyclopedia of Sea Horses," Mildred Bellomy aptly sums up the strange conglomeration that comprises the sea horse's appearance.

She says, "He has a tail like a monkey, a head like a horse, eyes like a chameleon, a body that is armor plated like an insect, and it is well supplied with skeletons, having one inside and outside."

It is no wonder the sea horse was a creature of fabulous legends and fables. Who, without concrete proof, could ever believe such an odd-shaped creature could actually exist--and still be so appealing.

# Chapter 3

## BEGINNING UNDERWATER PHOTOGRAPHY

### Underwater Cameras Are No Longer The Property of Only the Rich & Famous

Souvenir hunting is a favorite activity of many divers and snorkelers, but too often the treasured finds lose their appeal once out of the water. Artifacts may slowly crumble from being exposed to air and shells may lose their colorful luster.

When any of these things happen, the souvenirs are hardly what anyone wants to recall an exciting or memorable dive.

Though this may sound like a Kodak commercial, most experienced divers know that photos are the only thing that truly capture the mood of a sunken ship or the lively colors of a coral reef.

Underwater photo equipment no longer costs an arm and a leg. Each year, more and more options become available. Underwater photography is finally within the financial means of everyone. How much you spend depends on how deep you want to get into the subject.

Actually, it's possible to get around having to buy any new cameras at all by using a regular land camera in a specially protected housing made of high-impact Lexan. Placing a favorite 35mm camera in an underwater housing may seem risky, but housings have been on the market for decades and flooding is not a serious threat. Furthermore, housings have been refined to such a point they offer a photographer almost as much camera control underwater as he would have on land.

Installing a camera in a housing is simple. In most models, the first step is to fasten a clamp to the camera lens for focus control. The camera, secured in a tray, is then snugly fit into the housing. All that's left is to snap the housing shut; after that, the camera is ready to be submerged. A rubber o-ring around the opening provides the waterproof seal. Lubrication of the o-ring with a special grease provides added protection against water seeping in.

With a good housing system, a photographer can still frame his subject without the parallax problems associated with a top-mounted viewfinder, and he has the same precision for focusing. Most importantly, a photographer can use his full range of lenses. If he wants to switch from a normal to a wide angle lens, all he need do is change the plastic port or dome on the housing. For complete housing information, contact the largest manufacturer of housings: Ikelite Underwater Systems, 50 W. 33rd St., Indianapolis, Indiana 46208; 317/923-4523.

Still, there's an even cheaper housing option over the hard Lexan models--using flexible plastic bags for either autofocus or SLRs. Manufactured by EWA-Marine in West Germany, an optical glass lens is used for edge to edge sharpness; a built-in glove gives easy access to the controls. Called waterproof flexible housings, these soft housings come in a variety of styles that even allow the addition of a strobe, motordrive or even telephoto lenses on an automatic SLR. They're even available for video cameras and are capable of operating as deep as 33-55 feet.

However, when using an autofocus camera in an EWA housing, you do need to decide ahead of time how far away you want to take your photos. Without correction, the autofocus is sharp only from 7 feet to infinity. For between 2-7 feet--the ideal shooting range as will be explained later--a 2x or 3x closeup lens must be attached to the outside lens ring, which is no great difficulty. For complete information, write

*The easiest and most compact underwater camera system is the Nikonos.*

EWA-Marine, 216 Haddon Ave., Westmont, NJ 08108; or toll free, 800/ 257-7742.

While housings are fairly popular, undoubtedly the most used system is the Nikonos, the amphibious version of the Nikon. On the market since the 1960s, it still is the only professional quality underwater camera available. The camera body itself acts as the waterproof housing; no other protective covering is needed. Until the new auto-focus, the Nikonos' biggest drawback was having to estimate the focus distance. Since everything appears one-third closer underwater than it actually is, this wasn't always easy to do.

However, the new generation Nikonos is anything but a submersible box camera: technology has finally caught up with demand, as autoexposure and autofocus both are now available.

The newest model Nikonos is quite expensive, but you should be satisfied with the capabilities of the older models if you're most interested in shooting wide-angle subjects prominently featuring divers. For instance, tight focusing is not crucial if you use a 15mm since everything from about two feet to infinity will be in focus at f5.6-f8. The 35mm once sold as a standard package is useless for anything except closeup or macro photos.

A serious photographer is better off purchasing the body and a 20mm or 15mm lens. The 15mm is the ideal, but the price tag of the lens and viewfinder is over $1400, which puts it out of reach of all but serious professionals. The much less expensive 20mm is a good compromise.

Wide angle lenses work best for everything but fish portraits for a number of reasons. First, since there is less light underwater, you must get close to your subject to capture whatever color exists. By being closer, any sand or dirt in the water is less likely to show up.

For example, the amount of water and suspended particles are considerably greater at 8 feet, yet that's about what it takes to full frame a diver with the standard 35mm lens, while a 15mm or 20mm will do it from about 3 feet away.

An acceptable alternative to the Nikonos is the Motor Marine II by Sea and Sea, which sells for much less. The only problem will be finding one to examine since it's not produced by a major manufacturer. Like the Nikonos, the Motor Marine II is capable of going as deep as 150 feet. It not only has a built in flash but you can add a more powerful strobe from Ikelite for sharper, better illuminated photos.

Minolta and Vivitar currently offer fairly inexpensive amphibious cameras that are perfect for shallow water snapshots and snorkeling. Minolta's Weathermatic Dual 35 has the unique capacity to let you select a standard or wide angle lens simply at the push of the button, whether the camera is in or out of the water. No other camera in the world presently offers this feature. The camera, rated to a depth of 16 feet, is also perfect for river and fishing outings that might be too risky for a conventional SLR.

Minolta's autofocus feature works only on land but uses a fixed focus underwater that prevents you from moving in too

*Even with a wide-angle 15mm lens, it's possible to get closeup pictures of fish.*

close. I own a Dual 35 but I've almost stopped using it because I don't think the pictures come out as sharp as they should.

Another good all-around camera to consider is Vivitar's TREK 50 which dives to 10 feet. Featuring a built-in flash, it uses a fixed focus lens but provides a special switch for closeup work.

Still another good compact camera for underwater work (though probably too cumbersome for easy land use) is the Hanimex 35mm Amphibian Camera. With motor drive and a powerful built-in electronic flash, it goes to an incredible 150 feet, same as the Nikonos.

Compact cameras with built-in electronic flashes have a definite cost advantage over the Nikonos and cameras secured in a housing. For anything more than silhouette shots below 15 feet it's necessary to have artificial light. Even the shallowest pictures tend to contain a blue or green cast without strobe light. This is because as light enters the water, it is refracted and separated into the different colors of the spectrum, and some of the colors start fading out at 10 feet. So, for serious photography, a strobe is essential.

It's much cheaper to buy a housing for a land strobe ($100-$200) than it is to invest in an amphibious strobe with comparable features ($600-$900). Better yet is a camera that already comes with a flash.

Still, despite its considerably greater cost, the Nikonos coupled with its extremely powerful TTL flash will outperform any of the other cameras listed. The question is whether you want to spend between $3,000 and $5,000 for a good professional outfit with 15mm lens, camera body and strobe.

In the final analysis, which system you choose shouldn't depend just on price. What's more important is how much you'll use your outfit. A serious photographer who dives regularly is likely to become frustrated and disappointed with anything less than a Nikonos or Ikelite-style system. On the other hand, the occasional snorkeler should be quite content with the compact autofocus variety.

## Video Cameras

No doubt about it: pictures that move are a lot more interesting to view than slides or prints. And thanks to the variety of tailor-made camcorder housings, any diver can re-experience the action of his dive trips anytime he chooses.

Camcorders have several distinct advantages over still cameras. Most importantly, the camcorder can take natural light pictures when Nikonos shooters must use a strobe. Further, the continuous video action often compensates for shots that don't turn out perfectly. Shots that would be thrown away on slides or prints turn out well on video because backscatter or awkward camera movement are only temporary distractions. On a still photo, either would destroy a picture.

Naturally, you need to become proficient with a camcorder on land before you can expect to take quality footage underwater. The key to success is to experiment on land with every possible setting and mode and learn from the results.

With rare exceptions, good pictures don't just happen. They require intimate knowledge of your equipment. Even shots that seem to be the result of nothing but luck are often based on considerable skill. Confronting a lucky situation

*Artificial light is usually necessary below 20 feet unless you want to take silhouette shots. Note how the hand lights illuminate the sponge, but everything else remains dark.*

(such as encountering dolphins in the wild) is one thing...being able to take advantage of it is something else entirely.

Only after you understand your equipment thoroughly should be think about getting it wet. Even then, as anxious as you may be, don't just jump in. Take plenty of pool time to become familiar with your housing. Problems with leaks are best resolved where the sickening discovery of tiny bubbles doesn't devastate the equipment. Test everything extensively before getting near salt water.

At poolside, read the housing instructions again thoroughly for any warnings about maintenance and proper handling. Test for leaks by placing the port in the water to see if any water collects. Then gradually submerge the housing, always keeping the side with the electronic board (if there is one) at the top so that if water enters it can never reach this crucial area. Once you're certain all is well, practice, practice, practice with how the camcorder interfaces with the controls.

This may seem obvious and overemphasized, but you'd be surprised at how many divers with new camcorders have trouble their first few times in the water.

## *Technique*

Always remember, the camera is there to record motion...not to be moved. There's no better way to make an audience seasick than to show a video where the photographer always zooms in and continually pans the scenery. Everything becomes a mindless blur.

Some general suggestions on how to avoid these problems:

1. Begin with a wide-angle long shot. This establishes where you are, what the terrain is like: whether it's reef or wreck, salt or fresh water, night or day.

2. A medium-shot begins to emphasize the points of interest by eliminating the nonessential. Your main subject is far more prominent than in the long-shot. The medium-shot is the one most favored by the majority of underwater photographers.

3. Next, move to the closeup next to show the dramatic details of your subject. Highlight the creature or the diver. If

you don't, you'll be keeping the viewer distant from the action, which is frustrating. It's like seeing the details of a dive watch in a jewelry store from outside the window.

4. Back to the medium-shot.

This sequencing can certainly be altered. If fact, you'll generate more interest if you shift the order. Change the camera angle when possible at the start of each sequence for even more variety.

How long should each shot run? Unless the action is incredible, 10 seconds is the recommended maximum, with an overall of 15-20 seconds for any one scene, regardless of the number of shots.

## Lighting

Natural sunlight is all you need for most wide-angle shots. However, you need to compensate according to depth for the best possible color.

Several general rules:

- Use the filter supplied by the housing manufacturer or a UR-Pro filter anytime you rely on natural sunlight.

- Above 20 feet, the colors may run too red unless you set the color balance for indoor. In very bright conditions, set the shutter speed for 1/100 second or higher to prevent burn out.

- From 20 to 60 feet, set the color balance for outdoor.

- Below 60 feet, leave the color balance set for outdoor and remove the filter. In dark water, set the shutter for 1/60 second to increase depth of field.

Added light is essential for good closeups and of course for night dives. For even lighting, it's best to mount two lights instead of one. The power needs:

- for macro, 50 watts

- for subjects 1-3 feet away, 100 watts

- for subjects 2-5 feet, 200 watts

- for subjects 5-8 feet, 300 to 400 watts

*35*

Both still and video photography require patience and practice. However, you can increase your expertise dramatically by enrolling in one of the Nikon underwater camera schools or taking place in one of the Nikonos Shootouts, a combination vacation/competition/seminar package.

NIKON SCHOOL OF UNDERWATER PHOTOGRAPHY: Week-long intensive sessions are held year-round at top dive resorts and live-aboards throughout the world. The teachers vary according to location. For information, call 800/272-9122 or 305/451-2228.

NIKONOS SHOOTOUTS: Also held in exotic destinations throughout the year. Write Nikonos Shootout, Box 2487, Key Largo, FL 33037; 800/272-9122.

# Chapter 4

## EASY MACRO PHOTOGRAPHY

### Even the Smallest Creatures Loom Large

Think small. That's the way to take some of the most striking and colorful underwater photographs. The skill and equipment involved are such that almost anyone can produce expert results with the first click of the shutter.

Macro-photography is the formal name given to this special photographic technique. It involves taking pictures of very small objects, only one to three inches across, or selected sections of larger ones.

For such pictures it's necessary to have your camera about six inches away from your photo subject. That automatically eliminates some photo subjects--such as an approaching shark. Still, there are more opportunities for pictures of fish and other moving objects than you might think.

Most divers soon realize that most of the colorful marine life worth photographing, aside from fish, is quite small. Yet most camera lenses will not focus closer than two or three feet from the subject. This is much too far away to show the details of intricate coral patterns or small crabs and other animals. However, it is not necessary to invest in a lot of new camera equipment in order to take close-ups if you already have a basic underwater camera.

This discussion will be limited to close-up systems appropriate to the Nikonos, the underwater version of the Nikon. Two close-up systems are available for use on the Nikonos. Before deciding which one to buy, you must ask yourself several questions: (1) Are my pictures for publication, or are they simply for the enjoyment of myself and my friends? (2) How many underwater cameras do I eventually plan on investing in? (3) Am I willing to shoot nothing but an entire roll of macro-photos without the possibility of taking other kinds of pictures of objects that may suddenly present themselves-- such as that approaching shark?

The simplest method for macro photos involves placing an extension ring--actually nothing more than a metal collar-- between the camera lens and body. This extension ring allows the camera to focus much closer than it otherwise could. In fact, true macro allows you to take life-size pictures of the smallest creatures.

However, once this extension ring is on the camera, it cannot be removed without surfacing, drying the camera off, removing the collar and screwing the lens back on. All that takes valuable time. Realistically, once the close-up system is mounted for a particular dive, it's never removed.

This can be frustrating if there's something else you suddenly want to take a picture of but can't.

I was once taking close-ups when I noticed a resting sea turtle. I've been trying for years to get good shots of sea turtles, but they are usually difficult to find, much less get close to.

To reassure myself that this particular turtle wouldn't have let me get close to him if I'd had the proper set-up, I swam slowly toward him. I almost got within touching distance before that turtle swam away; and I have yet to get a good turtle picture.

If you can afford it, the obvious solution to this dilemma is to carry a second camera. But the cost of a second camera body and lens is more than most divers care to spend.

A good compromise is a close-up lens that simply fits over the regular camera lens. You can remove it underwater with

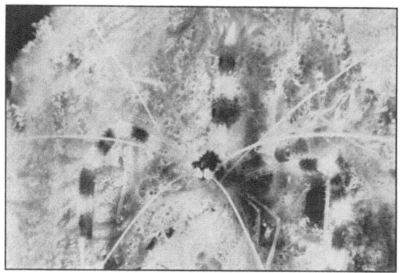

*The red and white candy-striped banded coral shrimp is a favorite macro subject.*

no problem. If you find a subject that requires a close-up attachment, you simply slip on the close-up lens. When it's time for a regular photograph, take it off.

Unfortunately, not all attachment lenses provide pictures as sharp as those taken with the extension rings. The photos are fine for projection, prints and so on, but not always good enough for publication. Also, you usually can't focus closely with the attachment lens.

I prefer the extension ring system because of its greater focusing ease. A set of removable frames is normally attached to the extension ring. The frames work just as the name implies: a three-sided oblong frame extends out from the camera to include exactly what area the camera lens will cover.

To take a picture, all you do is place the frame around your subject and fire the shutter. The guides which attach the frame to the extension ring automatically determine how close your camera should be to your subject.

In close-ups, the proper distance of your camera from your subject is critical. Since there is very little depth of field,

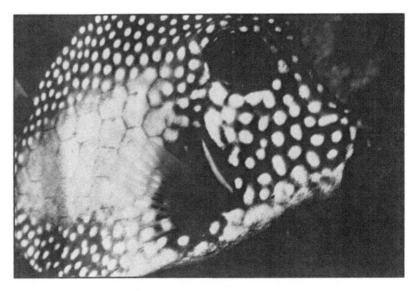

*This trunkfish was photographed with a 1:3 macro frame.*

you have little margin for error. With the attachment close-up lens, you have to estimate where to place your camera. Since everything appears much closer underwater than it actually is, you may not be as precise as you need to be.

It is possible to buy small distance guides, called wands, to attach to the camera viewfinder bracket when using an attachment lens, but then you don't have room for a viewfinder for regular photographs, which defeats the whole purpose of this system. (True, you can still frame your picture via the built-in viewfinder in the camera, but this may be awkward to accomplish quickly while wearing a mask.)

Once you've selected your lens set-up, there is still the matter of artificial light. Because the different colors of light do not penetrate very far into water, beyond a depth of 20 feet or so, everything has a kind of bluish hue. Artificial light of some sort is necessary to bring out the vivid, dramatic colors predominant in the underwater world, unless you're diving in very shallow water.

The Nikonos is available with a strobe just for macro photography. If you don't already have an underwater strobe or don't feel like sinking $400-$800 into one, the easiest and

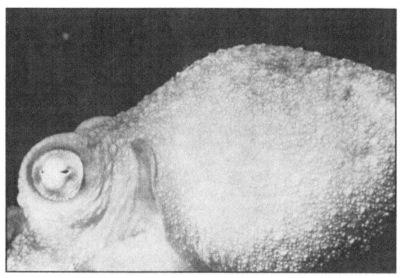

*Only part of this octopus fit inside the Nikonos closeup frames.*

cheapest method is to take your topside strobe down with you by acquiring a special housing and a connecting insulated wire from the strobe to the camera.

Your light source must be placed very close to your subject, since the lens is shut down to f-22 for its full focal length. If you're adapting a topside strobe to a housing, you'll need to experiment to see what distance provides the best illumination.

In all instances I hold my strobe off to the side and point it down. This gives an even distribution of light and minimizes the reflection of any particles in the water.

Which brings up another advantage of macro-photography. Because the camera is so close to the subject, you can film under almost any conditions, even those in which regular photography would show nothing but sand and mud. This is essential for photographing in harbor areas where the water is normally dirty, but where you'll also be amazed at what you'll find growing on the side of the pier pilings.

Macro-photography will also start you looking at the underwater world in a different way. As you search for photo opportunities, you'll become much more aware of the variety and interrelationship of marine life.

Even the ugliest-looking coral has intricate patterns missed by the average diver simply swimming by. You'll also come to notice the multi-colored shrimps, the fierce-looking but harmless arrow crabs, the tiny fish that live in the sea anemones, the countless other fascinating, beautiful marine creatures that are always present if you but seek them out.

One of the most exciting aspects of close-up photography is it can be done at night, when the delicate soft coral polyps extend to feed. Inspecting the different coral polyps in a selection of slides is like a trip through Fantasia. You can really see this best through macro-photography.

It's also possible to take close-up pictures of fish with a macro unit. It certainly isn't the easiest thing to do, but it can be done. There are two ways this can work. One is to center yourself in a school of fish while someone else is feeding them. At diving resorts, where the fish are fed regularly and are used to divers, it's not difficult to get them in your frames. However, they will be moving fast. There is a lot of guess work and luck involved in getting a good picture.

The other time for fish pictures is after dark, when the fish are asleep. Then you can come close enough to fish to touch and photograph them. It's amazing, though, how sleeping fish can suddenly come to life and leave you with nothing but an empty frame.

As with any type of photography, you need to vary your technique or the pictures will all begin to look the same. The natural tendency of most divers is to take nothing but horizontal pictures and place the subject squarely in the middle of the frame. Vertical shots, pictures with the subject diagonally in the picture or off to one corner, all lend variety and make your pictures more appealing.

Also, because there are so many interesting creatures that inhabit shallow, brightly-lit reefs and sandy ocean bottoms, it's not even necessary to know how to use scuba to take close-up pictures. Snorkelers will find more than enough to keep them busy.

For a different view of the ocean both photographically and visually, think small. Think macro.

# Chapter 5

## COLLECTING AND PRESERVING ARTIFACTS

### Steps to Take So the Memories Won't Fade

For divers, souvenir hunting seems as natural as breathing, and understandably so. It's the one hobby we can all enjoy close to home regardless of how poor the visibility or how cold the water temperature. What was discarded junk or the product of an unfortunate accident is for us apt to be a much-sought-after treasure: a ship's wheels, civil war buttons, old china and silverware. Prizes like these are still to be found in lakes, many inland rivers and off both coasts.

Unfortunately, the days of easy pickings are definitely over unless you happen to come across a previously undiscovered wreck--and that does still occasionally happen. But a lot of time can be wasted looking for new wrecks that could be more productively spent fine-combing the known sites for artifacts overlooked by previous collectors.

It's been said there is no such thing as a totally picked-over wreck, and that's true. The more obvious artifacts may have already been removed, but it's always possible to uncover more if you know how and where to search. This requires some of the same painstaking work of an archaeologist or paleontologist to sift through your particular layers of submerged history; and like a scientist, you need to be patient and thorough and not give up if you don't strike pay dirt every time. It always helps to look at it this way: you're eliminating the unproductive areas and getting closer to a satisfying find. For the most part, the main tools required for wreck excavation are only your hands. The most basic search technique in artifact collecting is known as "mudding." With one hand, firmly plant yourself on top of or beside the wreck so you won't float away. With the other, begin to slowly fan the sand, silt or mud until a small hole or cavity forms. As in gold panning, the useless debris is washed away and the heavier, more valuable objects remain. This simple method can uncover all sorts of artifacts: metal buttons, keys, china and silverware, anchor chain, possibly even the anchor itself.

The reason mudding works so well is that most divers don't take the time to fully investigate a wreck. If something is not out in the open, they typically figure nothing's left. As you'll discover yourself, they are so wrong.

With the whole exterior of a wreck to choose from, it may be difficult to know where to start. Several general types of locations are likely to be the most productive. Obviously, anchors and anchor chain are most apt to be found near the bow. Also look near hatchways, doorways and portholes where items may have fallen as the boat impacted the bottom. At sites where there is current, always work down current, which is where artifacts are most likely to have been swept. Remember, too, that what is available to you on the outside of a wreck continually changes. Storm surge may shift a wreck or the terrain around it. Portions that were inaccessible one year may be completely exposed the next, and vice versa.

In mudding, it usually gets too crowded if two divers work close together. Fins and arms tend to get in one another's way, and two people also make the water twice as mucked up. Always be aware of where your buddy is and what he's up to, but also maintain a discreet distance.

A good illustration of how effective this technique can be is a well-known wreck off the coast of the Yucatan, a Spanish galleon that was salvaged over 300 years ago for its precious cargo. The wooden timbers of the ship had long rotted away, and the site is in only 3-6 feet of water at low tide. Further more, the location is visited regularly by divers from a nearby

*Shipwrecks should always be entered carefully, with the way out readily accessible.*

resort. This has to be the prime example of what's thought to be a picked-over wreck.

Yet when I visited, I was able to uncover sizable quantities of glass beads and metal crosses (mostly in pieces) simply by fanning the sand, particularly the pockets inside the coral and rock-covered bottom. The slight surge didn't make it easy to remain in the same place without a bit of a struggle, but overall it was fairly easy work.

To be sure, nothing I found had any monetary value, but how many other divers have artifacts from an old Spanish galleon they have uncovered themselves--and done it so easily?

If mudding was able to uncover items there after more than 300 years of picking, it can do it anywhere.

I have also used this technique on Civil War wrecks in Virginia in water so black we did most of our work by feel. Where clarity is poor to begin with, mudding kills what little visibility there is, so it's necessary to pause occasionally so you can see what you've been doing.

If you become serious about artifact hunting, you may want to consider investing several hundred dollars in an underwater metal detector. They'll help you range out farther away from a wreck than if you were using simply your hands for your only search tools. In addition, they make it easier to search out new sites for possible wrecks. The manufacturers and costs are listed in any of the national treasure-hunting magazines.

Working the interior of a ship calls for a more varied approach but still the same basic technique. Assuming no artifacts remain in plain sight, start in the crew's or captain's quarters, the wheelhouse or the galley if you know their locations. Depending on the age and condition of the wreck you may not be able to identify these different parts of the ship until you start poking around.

If the ship is at an angle (and most are), begin by investigating the corners against the bulkhead on the downward side of the wreck. This is where artifacts normally end up after falling to the deck and settling after impact. Again, if none are visible, start mudding.

*Most wrecks list at an angle. Artifacts usually drop to the lower corners.*

This time, however, be very careful about how much you cloud the water since there is the important matter of finding your way back outside. When visibility starts to become poor in one section, move well away to another and start fanning there. Keep moving, working different locations, until things clear up at your original site so you can begin the rounds again. This permits you to cover considerable territory safely.

Obviously you should work out a plan with your buddy in advance to ensure that visibility inside the wreck is maintained. Tight quarters may require one person to remain outside to fan or stay at a hatchway and serve as tender while the other (tied to a safety line) goes inside.

As soon as an artifact becomes visible, the natural inclination is to free it completely with one big tug. With metal objects that may be safe, but it's best always to fan away all the silt or mud before attempting to free anything. Otherwise you could break a piece of china, rip apart a piece of cloth--destroy the efforts of your labor. It's a sickening feeling when that happens. All the wishful thinking in the world won't return the artifact to its original state; keep in mind patience always prevents damage.

Bulkhead corners are not the only parts of a wreck which may also be hiding (and protecting) artifacts. Peer under beams, steel plates, rocks, useless debris...anything. In the chaos of sinking, it's impossible to know what might have landed where. Don't hesitate to move things around, but never move anything that's acting as a support. Otherwise you might end up as an artifact yourself.

Once you've successfully located your artifacts, your task is only half-complete. You still need to preserve the item or restore it more closely to its original condition. For some artifacts, immediate action is crucial.

As destructive as its effects can be, immersion in salt water actually slows down the oxidation of some objects, which will begin to deteriorate quickly once they're exposed to air. Items that have been in the water for extended periods may be beyond hope.

Salvaged artifacts made of iron should be treated this way: first, remove any outside layers of oxidation or shell growth by gently tapping with a hammer. Next, rinse the item in fresh water, and then place it in a container of fresh water for about a week, changing the water daily.

After a week, the item is ready to be dried out by subjecting it to a 200-degree temperature for about three hours. A conventional home oven works nicely unless you have something unusually large.

Once it's been dried, go over the artifact with a wire brush. Your final step is to coat it with a clear sealer--such as a clear acrylic used for many tables--to end any possibilities of further deterioration.

Wooden objects also require special handling or it will end up with as many cracks as a shattered windshield. Wood that has been submerged for more than 10 years is wet all the way through and must be dried slowly to avoid cracking. For proper drying, the item should be kept damp (but not immersed) for 3-6 months. Only after that is it ready for restoration, which is accomplished by soaking the wood in a half-and-half solution of linseed oil and turpentine. If the

*Most of these items, including the buttons and sword hilt and other items, were recovered from a Civil War wreck in Virginia. Visibility was 1 to 3 feet.*

artifact is too large for this, you'll need to continually paint it with the linseed oil-turpentine solution until the wood stops soaking it up.

Now, the item is ready for display. The soaking solution imparts a rich dark finish and prevents further cracking.

China and glass items require nowhere near the same careful attention. A bath in fresh water will effectively remove any sediment. If you have a problem with calcareous growth, apply muriatic acid (the same thing used in swimming pools) to remove encrusting material. The acid works effectively without any damage. If you've been fortunate enough to locate some very old bottles, you do run the risk of having the glass start to flake on you. Spraying the item with a clear acrylic plastic will prevent that, but it may also destroy any monetary value the item has.

Brass and copper are among the most desirable items to find because they typically require the least amount of restoration work. If the item is retrieved from fresh water, virtually nothing need be done to it except polish it to bring back the original luster.

If it has a calcareous growth, muriatic acid will also effectively remove it without damage. However, this method does not work on chrome-plated items (like sink fixtures) since the acid will eat away the finish.

To clean either a brass or copper object, begin by placing it in a plastic container--do not use metal since that could leave a zinc coating on your find--and pour in enough acid to half-cover it. Using a pair of rubber gloves, turn the object so the acid comes in contact with all parts of it. You don't really need to soak it since the acid will start fuming and bubbling away on contact with the calcareous growth.

Make sure, too, you're doing your acid dipping outside or in a well ventilated area. Your container may start frothing like a witch's brew and the fumes can be harmful.

After all the bubbling has stopped, rinse the artifact in fresh water and baking soda to remove all traces of the acid. Next, while the metal is still wet, use a wire brush to eliminate the dark patina left by the acid. The polishing you can do yourself with a buffer or let a professional do it.

Artifacts collected and restored in the proper manner obviously are excellent decorations and nicknacks. They also let your friends know immediately you are a diver of considerable experience.

One word of caution in all this. If you are fortunate enough to find a wreck of true historical importance, double-check your procedures with a professional archaeologist at a nearby university. He may have a better method of preservation for delicate or truly valuable items. Who knows, you may even want to share your find with him so part of it can go on display in the university collection.

That kind of permanent sharing can be as exciting as the initial discovery itself.

# Chapter 6

## THRILL OF NIGHT DIVING

### Meeting Things Without
### Going Bump in the Dark

As we swim just a few feet over the reef top, I realize how appropriate our setting is for a science fiction thriller. Our light beams that cut through the particles suspended in the water have the appearance of laser rays intent on destroying the delicate marine life living below. It's like something from the old Orson Welles "War of the Worlds" broadcast, and I seem to be starring in one of the alien roles.

Which, of course, I am. It's at night a diver fully realizes just how inhospitable an environment the sea can be and how vulnerable he is. Many divers, understandably, are apprehensive about diving at this time, surrounded by total blackness.

Sight is limited to the narrow beam of your light; black space surrounds you; nothing is visible; you feel that anything could be waiting. The only way to know is to keep swimming ahead--with an occasional check behind. A swim through the sea at night can be a journey through all the primitive fears of the human race.

But that's only a first impression, and it is for the most part deceiving. Statistically, no more diving accidents happen during the night than in the daytime. The opportunity for increased danger is certainly there, but with a more serious attitude and a caution that is often lacking when the ocean is brighter and friendlier-looking, the likelihood of accidents decreases.

Anyone who scuba dives or snorkels will at some point want to try night diving. For one thing, this is the time when fish are most approachable as they rest near the bottom. On coral reefs, the true corals themselves emerge only after dark. The hard limestone rock of the reef is actually the shell of the soft-bodied animals known as polyps. The polyps usually do not emerge from their hard skeletons during daylight unless it is exceptionally overcast.

But at night they do venture out, and for the same purpose as other members of the reef community: food. The polyps' different shapes and colors (red, blue, orange) are amazing.

Sea anemones, looking like snake-headed Medusas of mythology with their many tentacles, are plainly visible on the coral and in the sand as they feed, continually moving food toward their mouths with the precision and determination of an orchestra conductor.

The anemones look fearsome and, to creatures their own size, they are. Anemones capture their food by stinging it to death. However, if a diver touches the poison-laden tentacles, he won't feel a thing; his skin normally doesn't even become irritated from the contact. Occasionally among the anemones you can find a cleaner-shrimp living among the tentacles. These shrimp, immune to the anemone's sting, are fascinating to watch as they perform their cleaning chores. It's other fish--not the anemone itself--the shrimp is involved in cleaning.

Amidst the long, waving tentacles of the anemone, the shrimp waits for interested fish to present themselves. To arouse their interest, the shrimp often waves its long white antennae. When a fish arrives, the shrimp climbs aboard and begins cleaning detail, entering the gills, mouth and even going between the teeth to remove excess food particles. Cleaner-shrimp, incidentally, are not supposed to be taken advantage of by their clients. Although everything in the sea likes shrimp, the cleaners are off limits.

*After the sun goes down, diving becomes far more interesting and more colorful.*

*Night is a particularly good time to photograph fish.*

After dark, armies of sea urchins also seem to invade the reef area. They are always present. At night they are on maneuvers, more visible, in their search for food. While it is normally the black sea urchin that's spotted during the day, at night pure white albino urchins and those with fudge-royal type spines are sometimes crawling the reefs. Yes, at night even a sea urchin can be beautiful.

Also seen normally only at night is the basket starfish, a creature which looks too fragile to be a living organism. During the day it hides among the soft corals, looking like a frazzled scouring pad. After dark when it extends its arms to feed, it is like a large surrealistic Christmas tree ornament with many fine webs connecting the pencil-thin points. If you didn't know better, you could mistake this starfish for an underwater spider web.

The darkness also draws out fish species you seldom see during the day. Probably the most notable are the spotted drum and high-hats, two small species distinguished by their long dorsal fins and black horizontal stripes. Even at night the

*Mom and Pop scorpionfish blending in with the coral. Their camouflage makes them especially difficult to spot, even at night.*

fish are extremely skittish and can usually be found only by looking under ledges and tight overhangs. The high-hat is a collector's prize, which may account partially for its rarity. Its dorsal is unique, like a fashionable hat worn by ladies of royalty in the Middle Ages, with a cone-shaped design and a trailing veil.

Far more common, and a much better photographic subject, is the smooth trunkfish, which is a misnomer if ever there was one. The fish looks a lot like a deflated puffer dotted with Liquid Paper. It is usually very approachable as long as you don't move too quickly, and an ideal subject for close-up pictures. Blown up on a slide, its lips are very distinctive, almost like a kissing gourami getting ready to pucker up.

Probably my own favorite encounter at night is with the potentially dangerous scorpion fish, which is usually too well camouflaged during the day to spot. The scorpion fish spine carries a venom which can be quite painful. The fish don't attack but are stepped on, even sat on, by clumsy divers. I saw one diver almost grab one, mistaking it for a piece of coral or bottom debris. Instead, this fellow put his hand down about four inches from one of the fish resting in the sand. It never moved. If it had the disposition of an angry moray, the results for the diver might have been disastrous.

I am fascinated by the eyes of scorpion fish. Under a light they sometimes become cherry red, like those of a man who has consumed too much whisky. Usually the fish will stand still for such close inspection. However, I have had them get irritated and swim up toward me to drive me away. One came very close to grazing my stomach with its spine as it made a sudden bolt into the darkness behind me. Since that incident, I do more of my viewing from an arm's length.

To keep from getting cut or scraped while on night dives, it's customary to go in full dress; that is, long pants, and long sleeve shirt or a full wet suit. Some people even wear leotards for protection. Others wear jump suits or baggy clothes of any sort. One thing is certain, night divers will never be asked to take part in a fashion show--a rummage sale, yes.

Gloves provide protection in case you need to grab hold of something quickly. Most night divers carry at least two lights, the second one for a spare. With some underwater lights today as small as flashlights, it's no problem to stuff a full backup light inside a BC pocket.

Should your light go out, it can be an uncomfortable few minutes until you locate and turn on your other one. If your buddy's light happens to be temporarily hidden from view, you will get to experience a darkness of the type that does not exist anywhere on land out of doors. Despite what many mystery writers have said, there is no such thing as a pitch-black night. Outside, even when the heaviest clouds obscure the sky, there is always enough light to see at least your hand in silhouette in front of your face.

But underwater at night there is total darkness, a darkness so complete it is impossible to define the closest form. It is like being locked in a closet with all the door cracks sealed.

It can seem like an awfully long time until you get that extra light turned on. This of course is why there's an added feeling of safety in numbers. In the darkness, divers have a tendency to stay together. Your buddy will probably be more like a shadow than a separate entity. This is not only in case of trouble, but so the two of you can point out the many interesting creatures to one another.

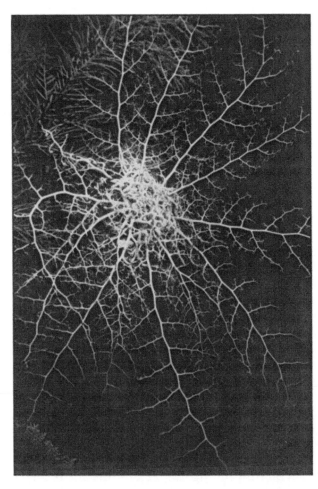

*The basket starfish extends to feed only at night.*

Still, it sometimes happens that divers do become temporarily separated. Usually that's only a temporary inconvenience as long as each buddy team has anticipated this in advance. If the two have talked it over beforehand, both should be surfacing at about the same time to regroup and begin again. If such an elementary precaution isn't decided before the dive, both divers could end up spending too much valuable time searching for one another. (This is a situation that rarely affects snorkelers.)

A few basic hand signals should also be verified ahead of time. They can be telegraphed by aiming the light straight across so it doesn't shine in your buddy's eyes, which will only serve to destroy his accumulated night vision.

Perhaps the one factor you can't plan ahead for on a night dive is a feeling of vertigo, of disorientation, that creeps over some people. They become confused about which way is up and down; their normal landmark bearings, hidden in the darkness, are missing, and a feeling of panic may start to set in. Should this occur, the exhaust bubbles indicate the direction of the surface. Even that won't always erase the continued feelings of uneasiness. In that case, the dive should be aborted.

Practically, as well as psychologically, it pays to have a helping hand back on shore or in the boat for after the dive. Someone needs to be available to make sure the beacon light left on the beach or tied to the anchor rope remains on to guide divers back in. A first-aid kit should always be kept handy for coral cuts. These wounds can take a long time to heal unless treated promptly.

The group discussion after a night dive is usually much more animated and excited than those which follow most day dives. Divers will be comparing notes on the different types of creatures they spotted and the photographs they hope will turn out. As contradictory as this might seem, it's the bright colors seen at night that generate the most comment. None of the various hues are filtered out by the water as happens in the day. The beam of a flashlight is far more efficient than the sun in this respect.

While at first impression diving at night may appear foreboding, perhaps even frightening, remember that statistically it's safer than your drive to the dive site. Once you've seen the ocean floor after dark, diving by day may seem tame and dull in comparison.

# Chapter 7

## STALKING THE WILY LOBSTER

### How To Put Lobster Within Affordable Reach

Locating lobsters is like finding a needle in a haystack: you want to rely on eyesight instead of feel, or the search could be painful.

After all, if you go sticking your hands into coral crevices for lobsters you might come out with a moray eel instead, and chances are you don't want one.

The lobster is the undisputed delicacy of the sea. It is craved by jewfish, octopus, skates and sheepshead and other predators which, in addition to man, dine on the tasty crustacean whenever possible.

Realizing its appeal is more than shell deep, the lobster has adopted the policy of many movie stars and taken to a sheltered reclusive life. As a result, snorkelers and divers will usually find lobster fairly difficult to locate. Normally all you see are the thin waving antennae protruding out from under ledges, crevices and holes and reef caves.

Just as grits, cornpone and good chili are peculiar to one part of the country, so it is with the spiny lobster. "Panulirus

*These lobsters are hiding under a coral crevice. Grab them only by the base of the antennae.*

argus," as it is formally known, is quite distinctive in its lack of claws, a prominent feature much coveted on its northern counterpart. This has both its good and bad points: it means the spiny lobster is easier to catch since you don't have to worry about your fingers getting crushed in a hearty hand-shake, but there's also less of the lobster to eat.

Unlike the clawed lobster, the spiny lobster comes in for a lot of bad names. Evidently since it doesn't have claws, people feel they can call him almost anything they want: crayfish, crawdad, bug. They believe if it doesn't have claws, it doesn't have class.

The spiny lobster normally migrates in the fall following spawning and molting. These mass movements can involve thousands of the creatures in Florida and Mexico after the first winter storm. Spiny lobsters seem compelled by some mysterious force to move to deeper water, forming long lines in the open as they travel, a movable feast for the diver lucky enough to find them.

Normally, however, you have to be content to take lob-sters one at a time around reefs, jetties, wrecks and artificial

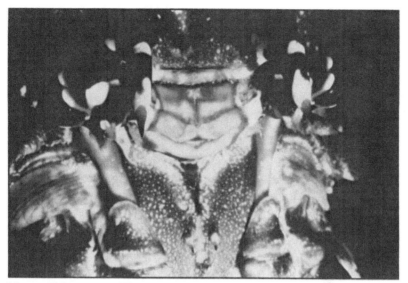

*Meet old bug eyes. This is a closeup of the eyes of a spiny lobster.*

reefs. Since artificial reefs are visited mostly by line fishermen, they can be well worth regular weekday visits when angling activity is minimal.

In shallow water, you can cover considerable lobster territory by dragging a snorkeler slowly behind a boat. Then, when a lobster is spotted, he simply lets go and descends to capture your meal.

Heavy cotton or nylon gloves are almost essential for either the spiny or clawed lobster. It's not that lobsters bite or anything, but the shell is sharp and can be unpleasant to grab.

The first time you spot a lobster, the natural urge is to grab the ends of the openly exposed antennae. That's fine if all you want is a matched set of antennae, which are too delicate to endure much manhandling and normally break off.

However, sometimes a lobster has to be nabbed by the antennae because it's wedged in too tight to reach him any other way. Grab it at the antennae base. Any higher up and the antennae will break off.

Lobsters, however, are fairly curious and not very bright, so if you haven't spooked one too badly you may be able to lure it out of its cave by cunning and guile.

How? Simply beckon to it with your finger while the rest of you stays motionless. The lobster may become curious enough about the movement that it will move from its hiding place so you can grab it. It sounds crazy, but it can work.

Although lobsters do move extremely fast when they snap backwards like a shrimp, an escaping lobster shouldn't be considered lost. While it may appear to be moving at jet speed, the burst often occurs only once and the flight path is normally in a straight line.

If a lobster gets free, swim after it as fast as you can. Before too long, you'll probably see it resting on the bottom (undoubtedly thinking nasty thoughts) or crawling along slowly.

To try again, approach slowly and distract the lobster's attention with one hand while you catch it with the other. Sometimes a lobster will remember it's seen that trick somewhere before and keep up a fast, steady retreat. In this case, you might as well give up unless you feel like some futile swimming practice.

Suppose your lobster doesn't want to play games but wants to stay at home. Then how do you dislodge it from its hiding hole? The obvious answer is to reach in and grab it with your glove-covered hand.

The only problem is that many reef creatures, including lobsters, sometimes have roommates, including types you wouldn't want to meet on a blind date: sea urchins, scorpionfish, moray eels.

On the other hand, you may discover a lobster has a sister or girlfriend and you find two where you had expected one. The procedure, in any case, is to indelicately grab the lobster by the head and pull strongly, twisting at the same time, to dislodge it. Or, if there's room, spread your hands, reach in the opening and grab.

Understandably, some people are squeamish about sticking an appendage in any place where it might be punctured or nibbled. For them (and I include myself in this group) there are several other methods equally effective.

If the lobster's hiding place has a sand or mud bottom, you can stir it up with your hand or an old broom handle. After

*Now you know why it's called a spiny lobster...and why gloves should always be worn.*

you've done this, get back to the edge of the muddy water. A lobster evidently doesn't appreciate water pollution and will usually leave its cave: grab it.

Lacking a dirt floor, you can try "tickling" the lobster. This is really a misnomer since it's doubtful a lobster feels anything funny through his shell.

In tickling, you take a blunted broom handle or stick and reach into the hole and tap the lobster on the shell. You shouldn't need to jab or gouge him to get him to come out.

If things that go bump in the night don't bother you, late evening or after sunset is perhaps the best time to dive for lobsters. At night, the spiny lobsters themselves venture forth in search of food. The creatures are actually scavengers, although, if given a choice, they will dine on other lobsters, sea urchins, crabs and other smaller crustaceans.

Since lobsters often move onto shallow sandy flats at night, netting (where legal) can sometimes be more efficient than diving. To net, you need a bully net, which has a long handle and a hoop attached at a right angle.

With a bully net you pole or drift quietly across the flats until your light either picks up the lobster or his orange-red eyes. Then you keep the light on the lobster and continue to approach quietly. When you're close enough, scoop it into your net.

Lobster laws have had a maddening habit of changing regularly in recent years, so always check locally for the latest size limit and the number of crustaceans you're permitted to keep. In most localities, you're not allowed to break off the tail until you've reached shore. That way if authorities should stop you, they'll be able to determine whether your catch is within legal limits.

One of the worst things to get caught doing is stealing lobsters from a commercial trap. If the law catches you, it's only a hefty fine. If the lobsterman catches you, it could be a bullet. That is no exaggeration.

Lobster is not only a delicacy, it is delicate and must be handled properly after capture to prevent spoilage. It should be kept cool in some way, either immediately put on ice, in a wet burlap sack or, best yet, in a refrigerator. Lobsters, like crabs, can sometimes be kept alive for several days in a refrigerator or ice chest.

Once a lobster dies, it should be cooked immediately or the edible parts removed. This last point is crucial if the lobster is to be kept from spoiling. Once a lobster dies, the digestive juices of the intestines and stomach seep into the tail and body meat, causing contamination. Save the legs, too, which contain some of the sweetest meat.

Assuming you cook a whole lobster by whatever method (we'll mention a couple of favorites shortly), this is how you make the most out of your catch.

Wearing a pair of your well-padded gloves, first twist the antennae off at the base. Then crack open the antennae for the appetizing chunks in the base. On the northern lobster, the claws and arms can be cracked open like walnuts.

To remove the tail, twist the lobster halfway and pull. To get the meat out, cut the underside of the tail with a pair of scissors or a sharp knife. Bending the tail backwards will split

*Lobster hunters admiring their catch. Tails should never be removed until after the lobsters are brought back to land.*

it open. After pulling out the tail meat remove the intestinal vein.

To extract the meat in the body, first unhinge the back shell. Next remove the stomach sac from behind the eyes. Everything else in there--the liver, the roe of the female, the white meat--is edible. Only the spongy gills are not. Don't forget also to crack open the lower part of the body. There's a lot of white meat in there, too.

On a large lobster, crack open the legs just like a crab's. You may find big chunks of succulent, very tender meat in the legs. Unfortunately, there's not enough to bother with on small, skinny-legged lobsters.

Lobsters can be cooked in any number of ways. The easiest method is boiling. You simply drop the live lobster into the boiling salted water head first, making sure you have enough water to cover the tail. Place a lid on and bring the water back to a boil.

Cooking time depends on the size of the lobster. It takes seven minutes for a one-pound lobster, 12 minutes for a two-pounder, 15 minutes for one three to five pounds and about

20 minutes for a big bug going six to 10 pounds. Once cooked, the lobster should be placed under cold water for a few seconds, then served while still hot.

Broiled lobster is a favorite with many people. Trouble is when many first broil a lobster they make the mistake of leaving the lobster uncovered, which tends to dry it out. Make sure to baste it with butter as it cooks.

If there is a king of the sea, the lobster is it. The taste tells why.

# Chapter 8

## USING CURRENT
## TO YOUR ADVANTAGE

### Breezing Along Underwater

Clawing down an anchor rope hand over hand as your fins trail behind like flags flapping in the wind is the textbook illustration of a scuba diver's worst problem: current. Having to grope toward the bottom with all the effort of a mountain climber dangling at the end of a rope is enough to make most divers call it quits at the start.

After all, once on the bottom, your prospects probably won't improve: forward movement will be limited to inching ahead with your hands, elbows and knees, a reversion to the toddling playpen days before you could walk.

Spearfishing, photography and sight-seeing are almost impossible under such conditions. You can't really enjoy yourself if you're expending that much effort to stay anchored and not float away like a scrap of tissue.

But diving in current is like this only if you let it be in charge--if you waste your energy fighting it instead of harnessing all that water power on your behalf. Actually, diving in current can be one of the most pleasurable ways to dive once you start using current to your advantage.

Although more popular among scuba divers, drift diving also is a technique appropriate for snorkelers and free divers.

Current can be an asset for everyone: nothing allows you to cover more territory with less effort than going with the flow.

For safety purposes, drift diving is always done from a boat. That way you don't have to worry about a long swim back to shore or worry where the current is going to take you. And if someone should need immediate assistance for any reason, all they need do is pop to the surface and be instantly taken aboard; the boat always follows close at hand.

Drift diving also requires that at least two people stay on board, one to operate the boat and the other to lend a hand as people get out of the water. However, that doesn't mean they lose out on all the fun, since they can buddy up and head below once the first group is finished.

For the drift dive itself, the boat is kept in neutral with the engine running. Depending on how flat the water is, the boat may be able to follow the divers' bubbles. If it's too choppy for this kind of sighting system, one diver should attach a line and float to himself so the boat captain can track everyone's progress. If the current is slight, it's important that no one lag behind or there can be massive confusion in trying to round up everyone at the end of the dive.

An ideal drift dive is one where the current runs fast enough to let you skim over the bottom but not so strong that it requires a lengthy fight to attain depth. Too much of a struggle to get down is apt to make you exhausted and uncomfortable. It may also make you feel like you're in the midst of an endurance contest, forcing yourself to stay down just long enough to use up your air. Fortunately, there are few areas where currents are this bad.

How to describe a drift dive? In moderately strong current, it can be one of the wildest rides you'll ever go on; no amusement park has anything like it. I still vividly recall my first drift. The divemaster's simple instructions on what to do seemed just TOO simple. He told us only to fall off the boat into the current and start swimming downward from the start. When he gave the signal to jump, I fell in with all the others, figuring he was sure to know what he was doing. He did.

At 50 feet, I glanced back at my companions who were "standing" vertically. Air bubbles mushroomed from their regulators like soap bubbles from a child's toy.

*You can't fight a current. Instead, go with the flow...drift dive.*

I'd often heard the term "caught in the grip of the current," but never really appreciated the description before: it was as if some benevolent gigantic hand was pushing us along. There was no question about going in any direction other than the one in which we were being shoved. To try and resist would have turned that friendly grip into a choking, strength-draining vise.

But this current was warm, steady, unthreatening. As I relaxed, the dive gradually became more and more effortless. We could swim diagonally up or down or even slightly to one side, but the main work was being done for us.

I imagine that a walk in space must be very similar. Instead of a cloud-covered earth rotating below our feet, we had a multi-colored reef spinning by. For the first time I got an inkling of what the astronauts have the opportunity to experience.

I couldn't help but marvel at the fish living on this reef. They seemed to be expending a lot of energy to stay in one place. I imagined those that were an edible variety had been reduced to nothing but gristle from all their built-up muscle.

Some fish, obviously more experienced, stayed in the shelter of the occasional coral mound.

At one point, we drifted over what looked like an eel garden of big morays. As we passed, the eels were quite content to simply watch us float by. Although their eyes were much too small to see, we could tell they were watching us from the way their heads followed our progress. Even in the current they were able to move in that famous way morays have: back and forth slowly like a pool cue being readied for a slam.

Our air was exhausted much too soon. We glided toward the top, surfacing several yards from our buoy. The boat was close at hand, exactly as it should have been. It pulled ahead to bring the stern in line with our drift while we bobbed on top of the waves like ping pong balls. The operator cut his engine and we climbed aboard.

After the dive, I was surprised at how chilled I was despite the relatively warm water. Because we were not putting out much effort, the rushing water rapidly removed our body heat. I've worn a wet suit or shorty on all subsequent drift dives.

Although photography can be difficult under these circumstances, it is definitely worth attempting. Macro photography is almost impossible unless you're able to grab onto a rock or piece of wreck to anchor yourself temporarily. However, that can also put you behind the rest of the group, so it's definitely not recommended in strong current.

Drift diving around wrecks usually has to be done on the fly unless you can duck inside the ship's frame, out of the current. Abruptly attaining such comparatively quiet and calm water is like slamming the door on a windstorm.

Of course you know it's still waiting for you once you poke your mask above the deck frame, but that's part of the game, too. Obviously, you can take advantage of the stillness inside a wreck to take macro photos of the tiny animals clinging to the sides.

The trickiest part in handling camera equipment on a drift dive is getting cameras safely back on board while contending with current. It helps to put out a shock line with a snap swivel to hang about 10 feet below the surface. That way you'll be

*To prevent possible camera damage, use a shock cord to lower and raise equipment, particularly in current.*

*Diver inspects a thick coating of marine growth on a sunken ship as she drifts by.*

free to concentrate on removing scuba gear and not have to worry about lenses getting smashed against the stern or boarding platform.

Once you're back on the boat, simply haul up the line with your cameras. A shock line also is a convenient method for getting cameras wet. After you fall over the side, all you need do is swim to the line and unsnap your equipment.

If you do a lot of drift diving, it probably won't take too long before you decide to change the complexion of your sport and drift after sunset. Floating over the ocean bottom at night can be tremendously exciting. Your field of vision is confined to the narrow beam of artificial daylight emanating from your lantern. Normally your light is pointed only a short way ahead so you can view the passing scene to its smallest detail.

As a result, you're continually charging into a dense black wall which hides...well, you can never really be sure until you get there. For experienced divers, that's part of the challenge and fun of night diving. For novices, it's the best reason in the world not to get wet after sundown.

Night drift diving calls for a few added precautions to make sure divers don't become separated. Ideally, no more than four divers make up a team, each one carrying a minimum of one light and having a Cyalume tied to their B.C. The Cyalumes, small pencil-sized plastic lights activated by breaking them, are also used to make the float line visible.

A night-time float line should be about 50 feet greater than the maximum depth and have big corks or fishing floats tied off about 20 feet from the bottom end so that none of the slack line becomes fouled on any outcroppings. Rather than tie the line to a diver, it's easier and safer to use a large shark hook (minus point and barb) that's placed under a strap.

At night before jumping in, it's not a bad idea to activate a Cyalume tied just above the shark hook. It is also advisable to tie a clear plastic jug about 15 feet from the shark hook and place two working Cyalumes in there. In this way, if people do become separated during the dive, the hook can be secured to a piece of the bottom and the Cyalumes will serve as a rallying point.

The person carrying the float is usually the one in charge of keeping track of everyone else since he's the most visible. It helps if the float man is one of the more experienced divers who won't get so caught up in the sight-seeing that he forgets to keep an eye on the others. Getting absorbed in all the fascinating sights is what causes divers to drift apart.

Understandably, some people avoid anything related to night diving because it seems too much hassle. I entirely agree--it does SEEM that way. While gearing up during the day never seems any bother, at night it feels like it takes forever and then once you're in the water you can't stay long enough to make it worth while.

But drift diving makes it all worth while: you can actually stay down longer when floating with the current since there's little need to expend much effort. That means your air supply lasts longer. Plus you get to see so much territory you feel like you've actually been somewhere. More dive time, more territory covered: all advantages of drifting that make a night plunge well worth it.

There are some people, however, who simply refuse to go into the water after dark. Since an extra crewman to help divers out of the water is always appreciated, anyone with real trepidations about a night dive should be allowed to remain aboard, unhassled.

After all, there's always the next day. They can join you then as you continue your lazy, leisurely drift through life.

# Chapter 9

## WINTERTIME POOL GAMES

### Stay Active Year-round, Weather or Not

Except for those who like cold water, high seas or diving under ice, winter is not the diver's friend. Slide and video shows can help fill this land-locked period, but divers mainly like to do one thing: get wet.

At first glance, the following pool games may seem silly or bizarre. However, they are proven winners for bringing people together. If dive shop owners or clubs near you have become too sophisticated for this sort of unorthodox activity, apartments and condos will often sponsor such events. So will singles groups.

### Bike Racing Underwater

Bicycling in the off months is a good way to keep your legs in shape until it's time to suit up once again. However, you can also combine biking with diving to create a contest that will have people talking for weeks: a bike race, underwater, in a swimming pool.

Forget about modern or expensive racing bikes for this immersed Grand Prix. Instead, the sponsoring dive club or store should have several old clunkers for contestants to use.

That way, no one has to worry about the condition their bike is in after the race is over. And no one is likely to achieve an unfair edge by practicing at home in their pool.

An underwater bike race is a great fund-raising gimmick as well as a terrific way to gain media publicity, especially from TV. When you call the media, let them know they'll be able to get all the pictures they want--but never have to get wet.

To accomplish this, you need to provide a 15 or 20-gallon all-glass aquarium that has a clear, clean bottom. Then, all the photographers have to do is shoot through the aquarium; the results will be almost as good as if they had a housing. That means they'll be able to cover the event, from the first splash to the final dash.

However, your help is essential in getting these "under water" shots. Here's how you can assist--and of course, you should rehearse this before the race starts so everyone has their role perfectly rehearsed.

Two people need to hold the aquarium for the TV cameraman. Since an empty aquarium floats, the tank will have to be held down and on its side by the two handlers. The photographer will get his best shots either by lying on the side of the pool and focusing down and to the side, or by standing waist-deep in the water and shooting toward the deep end.

Figure out ahead of time which position is best for your particular pool according to the way the race will be run. If this goes well, you'll have no problem getting coverage for other events that offer similar video opportunities.

Plan the race according to the number of bikes and contestants. If you have three or four bikes and as many as 20 participants, it will take several different heats for the finalists to be selected, with the winners of each heat facing one another for the final elimination. Or you can take the three or four cyclists with the fastest times overall and let them fight it out in a big grand finale.

If you have a large number of contestants, keep the heat distances short so spectators don't get bored. Have everyone race down the length of the pool and return only once--no more.

*Bicycle racing underwater may seem insane, but it can be done.*

For the championship, you might want to make your racers peddle twice as far to add to the excitement and suspense.

You may also want to add to have two levels of difficulty according to sex or age group. You accomplish this by having the bikers race either with or without fins. Fins create more resistance and also demand more balancing skill.

You will need to provide a team of safety divers to extricate those who get tangled up in their bikes and end up sprawled on the pool bottom. You can have your safety divers automatically help anyone who goes down, or keep them in reserve only for extreme situations.

If you plan this as a fund-raising event, you will want to charge a small admission fee for spectators and contestants alike. The overall winner definitely deserves a memorable trophy to mark the occasion--perhaps a plaque showing a fish sitting on a cycle, or a diver in full gear with bubbles streaming as he speeds atop his bike.

You may want to offer something practical as well, such as a new mask or set of fins. Or a free local dive trip...anything that will motivate divers to get involved.

## Halloween Cut-Ups

Pumpkin carving is as old as Halloween itself, but have you ever tried carving pumpkins underwater?

It may seem a strange idea at first--even a little crazy-- but it's another kind of party any dive store or club can hold to bring everyone back together again after the main dive season ends.

Typically, the pumpkin carving is only one element of a regular Halloween poolside party. Those who want to compete can, and those who want only to watch can do that, too. Divers in Texas originated carving pumpkin underwater, and a lot can be learned from the early pioneers who made some mistakes the rest of us want to avoid.

For instance, you want to scoop out the pumpkins FIRST-- and not in the pool--or everyone will end up swimming through a fog of pumpkin juice. Worse, pumpkin innards are especially good at clogging up pool filters because of all the strands.

To prevent this from happening, the party host should scoop out all the pumpkins in advance. Or have the competitors do it before they get in the pool. If you hold the competition in open water, you don't face this kind of problem.

You might even be surprised at how many fish the pumpkin mess attracts. At Florida's Crystal River, the fish go absolutely crazy.

*A proud snorkeler shows off her pumpkin carved underwater.*

Normally, the party sponsor charges a small fee of $3-$5 from every contestant. Then the competitors enter the water whenever they feel like it and start cutting up with no time limit. Each artist is allowed to take as long as he wants. The competition can be sanctioned using either scuba or snorkel. If it's done with scuba the tank will automatically set each contestant's time limit.

For best results, grease pencils or crayons are offered so the face can be outlined before the diver gets in the water. This allows a certain amount of the artistry so the competition doesn't become just a contest of underwater dexterity. Ghosts, bats, witches--all are appropriate subjects along with the typical Jack-O-Lantern faces.

Although a thin-bladed dive knife will work satisfactorily, the best way to carve the more intricate designs is with a small saw blade that art stores have for cutting up styrofoam. It will probably even be necessary to offer a few art lessons the first time. To carve something like a black cat or a bat, you draw in the figure outline, then carve out the area around it in a circular fashion so the bat or cat looks like it would be silhouetted when a candle is placed inside the pumpkin. You don't carve out the figure itself--only the space around it.

Once the carving is under way, it's advisable to have every one carve over a plastic trash can to keep the mess in the pool to a minimum. Or you can give each contestant a plastic trash bag to store chunks of pumpkin in as they sculpt.

Although it's up to the sponsor's discretion, prizes typically awarded include items like T-shirts, free air fills, a pumpkin pie or key rings. Once the pumpkin-carvers are finished, the pumpkins should be displayed around the pool and votes taken in the following categories:
- Ugliest Pumpkin
- Scariest Pumpkin
- Funniest Pumpkin
- Best Overall Pumpkin

If people are still fired up after the contest is over and want to stay in the water, you can move on to an underwater trick-or-treat competition. This can be done on either a team or individual basis.

The "treats" everyone goes after can consist of numbered golf balls or pennies. If you use golf balls, you can award prizes for the highest score or according to who collected the most golf balls.

If you use pennies, scatter about 500 of them around the pool and let everyone dive for as many as they can gather in a certain time period. Or have teams do it in relays. Either method works well.

*Signing up for an underwater turkey shoot. The dots on the target are worth different points.*

## Underwater Turkey Shoot

For years, civic organizations have sponsored Thanksgiving turkey shoots to gain publicity and funds. There's no reason why dive stores and dive clubs can't do the same thing.

The biggest problem in holding a turkey shoot is not attracting people--they'll come in flocks--but finding the right type of target. Normal paper targets fall apart after only a few minutes underwater, so you to make them yourself. Use so-called textbook-cover quality paper, a type of paper so thick it's almost like cardboard.

Your turkey target should have lots of different score spots all over its body. You can give 100 points for head shots, 5 points for a leg shot and so on. The winner is the person who shoots the highest score. If there is a tie, a shootoff determines the winner.

Backstop material is as important as the target paper. The backstop needs to be made of something hard, like wood, that the spear will not go through.

*An underwater tug-of-war will also keep divers wet and active during the off-season.*

A backstop can be circular or square in shape; either works well. To set it up in the pool, you'll need to put weight belts on two sides to keep it from twisting around. A couple of good floats attached to the top will keep the target floating upright. If you have as many as three backstops in place, the shoot will run smoother and faster.

That's all there is to it.

To make it more competitive and give everyone more of a chance, each contestant should be allowed to buy 3 targets when he signs up. How much you charge for the targets all depends on the purpose of the shoot--whether it's for charity (in which case you can charge more) or whether you are out to make money for your store or club. A fee in the $3-$5 range is typical. Remember, the more you charge, the better your prizes will have to be.

The format for a turkey shoot typically goes like this. Once a person buys his targets, he's taken to the pool and made ready to shoot. However, he's not allowed to handle the targets since some people might be tempted to punch out a hole or two and claim them later for scores.

Once in the shallow end, the contestant never handles the speargun until they're ready to shoot. At that point, they are handed the loaded gun and allowed to make their first shot. For maximum safety, the spear tip should be a blunt one, and only one long rubber used to supply power for the gun so it will be a soft shot.

Further, the spear should be tied to the gun in case of any wild shots. It's safest to use only one gun for the entire competition. That way there is no chance of losing track of where a loaded gun is.

To keep up interest and the competitive spirit alive, it's best to keep posting the 10 highest scores so each person knows where he stands. That way if someone is suddenly knocked out of top place he has the chance to purchase more targets and try again.

Mask and snorkel are all the dive gear necessary, which also opens the contest to non-divers likely to be attracted by all the publicity. In Florida, hundreds of people have turned out for underwater turkey shoots after stories appeared in the newspaper or on their local noon TV shows.

If your event is for charity, you might be surprised at the kinds of donations you can get for prizes. Restaurants typically support this kind of event so you can give away free dinners. Or you can award ribbons or trophies, whatever. With proper planning and careful attention, an underwater turkey shoot can quickly become an annual event.

# Chapter 10

## COPING WITH SEASICKNESS

### The Motion of the Ocean
### Doesn't Have to Feel Fatal

As many divers know too well, few things feel worse than the agony of seasickness--except maybe labor pains or getting kicked in the stomach by a horse.

Many a boat trip begun in high expectation has dissolved into an endurance contest as hapless divers and snorkelers have fought to retain their dignity, sanity and breakfast.

Seasickness usually begins with a feeling of nausea, as though you haven't eaten in a week. Your palms and forehead begin to sweat. The world seems to swirl around you, and no matter how hard you try you can't seem to get it to stop.

In severe cases, you may experience recurring bouts of vestibulo-vegetative reflex. More commonly, that is known as tossing your cookies or chumming the fish.

Seasickness is not terminal. As many stricken landlubbers have reported for countless centuries, "At first I thought I was going to die. Then, as time passed, I was afraid I wasn't."

On short trips, seasickness usually lasts until you're able to jump in the water or your boat returns to shore. Once everything stops rocking, the world becomes right again. It's as if you've suddenly recovered from every ailment you've ever suffered. You never felt so good.

Seasickness, which the French have more elegantly termed "mal de mer," has been around since the first boats, and it is likely to always be with us, according to Orlando, Florida, audiologist Charles Solomon.

"Man may have come from the sea but he was never intended to stand on top of it in rolling ships. A tossing boat is too foreign to normal sense of balance. But if you take the proper steps, you can lessen the effects and even build up a resistance to it," says Solomon, an ex-marine who spent 22 years being ferried around the world and who now specializes in electronystagmography.

In other words, he is an expert in dizziness and the problems associated with it. His past and current professions make him very familiar with the causes and consequences of seasickness.

"Seasickness is part of the larger problem known as motion sickness," says Solomon. "People who get sick at sea often are just as susceptible to becoming ill in a car or in an airplane.

"In all cases the cause is the same. People were designed to acquire their spatial orientation--or balance--with their feet firmly planted on the ground. Going to sea disrupts what a person is used to. If your body cannot properly adjust, you become ill."

While the problem may seem to be located in the pit of your stomach, motion sickness is caused mainly by the inner ear, where humans have both a hearing and a balance component. The organ in charge of balance, known as the peripheral vestibular mechanism, is actually a pitch, yaw and roll control just like those used in airplanes. It lets you know where you are in regard to your spatial orientation.

This organ, part of a closed hydraulic system, is especially sensitive to out-of-level movements and sudden turns of your head. "When your system breaks down--when the coordination between your ear, eye and other receptors falls apart sending messages to the brain--we have a situation known as vertigo or dizziness. This is what causes seasickness.

*The surest way to avoid seasickness is to dive from shore.*

"If you feel seasickness coming on, pick out a visual reference and fix your eyes on that distant point. That can often help get rid of the nauseousness or sickness," Solomon advises. By fixing on a distant object, you regain the visual reference that was denied when your world suddenly started rocking because the boat started rolling.

"Habituation is the only solution," Solomon advises. "Your body will eventually adapt to the rolling motion of the boat and you'll finally get your 'sea legs.'

Some lucky people get their sea legs in only a few hours. Others will be sick for days, possibly a week or more, and may never fully acclimate before the end of a short voyage.

Apparently, many believe that as long as they are in sight of land they aren't as likely to become seasick. Solomon says that is wishful thinking.

"Some individuals get seasick after a boat hits the first few swells, and that may be just within several hundred yards of shore," he says. "The only advantage to being in the sight of land is the chance to fixate on the horizon to reduce the dizziness."

Some persons have no problem with nausea as long as they stay on deck, but become ill as soon as they enter the cabin or go below. These same people are 'cured' as soon as they get back out in the open and feel a breeze in their faces.

"While a breeze might help orient you a little as far as your balance goes, you get sick inside a cabin because you've lost your distant visual reference points. You might not have been aware you were fixating on the horizon or something on shore, but that's what kept you from experiencing vertigo while on deck," advises Solomon.

Stay outside and stay on your feet--not sit--and you are more apt to recover, says Solomon. When you stand, you supply more input to your brain. You'll feel the roll of a boat better when standing, which should help your body better understand what is happening and enable it to adjust sooner.

## *Seasickness RX*

Check with your family doctor before you take any medication intended to reduce the activity of the peripheral vestibular mechanism, or the pitch, roll and yaw control organ in the inner ear. Dramamine, one of the best known nausea-fighting preparations and one of the most readily available, will probably make you sleepy. Bonine is a good substitute. Both must be taken several hours before boarding the boat; waiting until the symptoms appear is too late. The ear patches are not recommended for divers.

- GINGER: Recent studies have shown that 2 capsules of powdered ginger root can be more effective than any medication. Check at the health food store. Or, sprinkle a tablespoon of ginger on your food several hours before setting out.

- COKE SYRUP: Carbonated cola beverages are well-known stomach pacifiers.

- OLIVES & LEMONS: If nothing else works, sucking on an olive or lemon helps reduce the amount of saliva which contributes to the nausea by seeping into the stomach.

*Once at depth, the problems caused by the motion of the ocean usually disappear.*

- ACUPRESSURE WRISTBANDS: This is a time-honored remedy from the Orient. The wristbands have a button that is worn over the acupressure point inside each wrist. Pressing on the buttons helps clear up the nausea for some people. These are most readily available at boating supply stores.

- FIXATE ON SOMETHING: Once the boat is underway, it's best if you pick out a distant object to fixate on so the inner ear and the rest of the body do not start going haywire. This could be a horizon, a cloud, the mast of another ship, a star--anything that is available.

- AVOID UNPLEASANT SMELLS AND VIEWS (including the sight of others getting seasick). Odors and sights by themselves won't cause seasickness but they apparently do contribute. Even the sight or smell of food normally appealing can trigger an attack of nausea for someone already feeling uneasy. Disagreeable smells ripen the prospect of illness that much more.

- NEVER BARF INTO THE WIND: If you do become sick, remember to stay on the leeward side of the boat during all chumming operations. "There is no reason for panic if this happens," Solomon says. "It will stop as soon as you habituate yourself to it."

- AVOID AN EMPTY STOMACH: An empty stomach may seem the ideal way to stop calling for "Ralph," but Solomon and many others think it is better to keep something in it. "I believe it is best if you eat something solid but light, like toast or bread," he says. "Others say it's better to drink something, but I think liquid sloshing around in your stomach will make matters worse."

- GET WITH THE RHYTHM: Another important step on the road to recovery is to become more familiar with the motion of the ship and learn to work with it. "We live by rhythms," Solomon points out. "Learn to anticipate each motion of the boat and shift your weight to acquire the proper balance. Then you will be working with the ship instead of being two seconds behind every movement, which throws off your balance mechanism even more. That is how you acquire your sea legs.

- PRACTICE GETTING DIZZY: If you have a history of seasickness, spin yourself around in a chair until you become dizzy. Learning how to control your dizziness in that situation should help you stay in charge atop a boat deck or inside the cabin. Astronaut trainees are acclimated to motion sickness by being strapped into a moving chair guaranteed to make anyone spill their guts. Relaxation or meditation during these practice sessions helps control the unpleasant sensations.

Ironically, once you've mastered seasickness, you may notice a slight balance problem when you return to shore. Back on land, you still find yourself weaving to the roll of the ship, as if you're still standing on deck.

What happens is that the body, which finally learned to compensate with the roll of the boat at sea, now has to wait for the brain to catch up with your legs, which are now on shore. Annoying, waiting for all these body parts to get in synch.

# Chapter 11

## DOES DIVING HURT YOUR HEARING?

### Don't Live in a Silent World

One of my best friends is a dive guide in his early 50s. He can be a difficult person to talk to, and not just because of his crusty personality. I have to talk twice as loud to him as anyone else.

This fellow is a very active and healthy diver except for his hearing, which makes him seem more like a person in his 70s than his 50s. His hearing grows worse every year. I've wondered if he'll be able to hear at all when he is 70.

His condition started me wondering about myself and anyone else who spends a fair amount of time in the water. Does diving adversely affect our hearing? Will it cause hearing loss? Can anything be done to prevent it, or, like old age, does it creep up on you without anything you can do about it?

Dr. Tom Mullin is an audiologist and chairman of the Communicative Disorders department at the University of Central Florida in Orlando. He has done considerable study related to diving and hearing. He says we average divers have little to worry about if we exercise common sense.

In fact, some jobs or home activities pose a much greater risk of hearing loss than diving because of their noise levels. Punch press and cement block machine operators and riveters are far more likely to suffer hearing loss. So are people who are exposed for long periods to noise from motorcycles, air boats, some power tools and even lawn mowers.

Loud lawn mowers can be more dangerous to your hearing than diving? No wonder I've never liked yard work.

Dr. Mullin points out several ways divers might suffer a hearing loss if they're careless. The first is through the common ailment known as "swimmer's ear."

"Swimmer's ear is a fungal or bacterial infection in the outer ear. It is medically known as 'external otitis.' It's a frequent problem for anyone who spends a great deal of time in the water, especially in swimming pools," Dr. Mullin says.

"The symptoms are frequent pain and drainage or itching, though not necessarily any actual hearing loss. Continued exposure of the ear to water irritates the condition."

Dr. Mullin says that for an infection to survive in the ear, three elements are necessary: warmth, darkness and moisture. "We can't do much about the first two, but staying out of the water can eliminate the third. This, plus medical treatment, can prompt the condition to clear up in a week or two."

If you persist in diving with swimmer's ear, you may cause very serious trouble. You may get a perforated ear drum. If that happens, you shouldn't dive at all--possibly ever again. The perforation occurs from too much pressure on the ear drum; it may also cause a significant hearing loss. The best thing to do: stay out of the water until swimmer's ear clears up completely. And afterwards, take ear drops (Lomotrin) every time you go in the water (even the ocean) to prevent recurrence.

Dr. Mullin says active, long-term divers could suffer a hearing loss, but that they should not worry if that happens.

"Anyone who dives regularly for a considerable period of time will probably notice a slight hearing loss," advises Dr. Mullin. "This is because the ear drum becomes thickened over long periods of diving, causing a sluggishness of movement in this membrane."

*A healthy reef makes a racket like a Geiger counter. It's a sound you never want to stop hearing.*

This sluggishness may result in what is known as a conductive hearing loss. This only impairs hearing to a slight degree and is usually medically correctable. It is something that should be watched for through regular hearing tests.

Unfortunately, there is a third-type of hearing loss which so far is not correctable. It is a common problem among professional divers, but not sport divers.

Dr. Mullin explains: "Divers say that they're 'clearing their ears.' Actually, they're not clearing anything but simply equalizing pressure in the middle ear cavity with the outside pressure, which can be significant depending on the depth.

"The air pressure in the middle ear exerts a tremendous amount of pressure on the part of the ear known as the oval window, the link between the middle and inner ear.

"The inner ear contains several incompressible fluids. So what happens is that a tremendous amount of pressure is being placed on incompressible fluids. This tends to change the chemical makeup of these fluids and causes hair cell damage in the inner ear. Unfortunately, these hair cells are actually nerve endings.

"Once these nerve endings are damaged, nothing can be done medically or surgically to correct the situation. This nerve damage results in a high frequency hearing loss similar to that experienced by older people. You may be able to hear what is being said, but you cannot understand it," according to Dr. Mullin.

This type of hearing loss is permanent. Hearing aids offer little help. A diver with a nerve-connected loss normally asks people to speak louder so he can hear better but he may still not be able to comprehend, because the hearing loss is in the high frequency range."

All consonant sounds of speech are in the high frequency range; vowels are at the low end of the spectrum. Since approximately 90 percent of intelligible speech is formed from high frequency components, this type of hearing loss can be devastating.

In such instances, divers have the most difficulty understanding women and children since they have higher-pitched voices. In addition, damage to these nerve endings often results in a phenomenon known as recruitment, which causes loud noises to be unusually irritating. Hearing aids which amplify sound often cause afflicted divers to complain that everything is too loud and still they don't understand what's being said.

But such a condition NEED NEVER OCCUR in the first place. Persons frequently diving deep only need have a periodic check of their hearing to see if they are beginning to suffer impairment.

Dr. Mullin recommends that all divers should have a hearing check-up at least once a year, the same interval recommended for most routine physical examinations. More avid divers might want to have check-ups every six months. The typical MD cannot perform the proper hearing tests. Instead, it involves a visit to an audiologist or otolaryngologist who will conduct an electronic hearing test to see what degree, if any, of high frequency loss has occurred.

The test involves being placed in a sound-treated room and having different frequencies transmitted to you through a set of earphones. The audiologist records your hearing ability in the different frequency ranges. At many universities and community speech and hearing clinics these tests are provided for little or no charge.

If you find you are starting to lose high frequency hearing, Dr. Mullin advises you should probably stop diving. Otherwise, there is the possibility of becoming completely disoriented underwater, or going deaf. In rare, extreme circumstances, death might even result from contracting meningitis or other diseases resulting from a perforated ear drum and other abnormalities that could happen.

Never dive with a cold or any sort of ear infection, since the pressure may create all sorts of hearing problems. A small pin-hole (fistula) leak which causes fluid to ooze out of the inner ear could result in a severe hearing loss, dizziness, tinnitus (ringing in the ears) and--if ignored--will lead to permanent hearing loss.

What about diving with a cold or sinus condition if you use drying agents to eliminate excess drainage? A qualified 'yes' to this, says Dr. Mullin. However, some drying agents may cause drowsiness and should never be used when diving. Others do not cause dizziness and may be medically sound with you--IF you check with your doctor first.

"Any diver who uses common sense should never have any trouble with his hearing. The occasional sport diver has little to worry about. It's the professional diver who is most likely to encounter real hearing difficulties. Of course, the sport diver will, too, if he ignores ear infections and does not have his hearing checked periodically," Dr. Mullin reports.

Diving may damage your hearing just as it may damage any other part of your body--but only if you're careless enough to permit it.

# Chapter 12

## PLANNING A DIVING VACATION

### Make It No Problem, Mon!

Regardless of how many dive trips you take over the years, your first vacation will always stand out. Why so? Because that first special dive trip is usually the first attempt to live out those dreams and fantasies we all have.

That first diving vacation may take you to the reefs of the Caribbean or the fabled lagoons of Micronesia. Or perhaps a much closer-to-home visit to the coast of California or Florida. The destination doesn't have to be exotic to be enjoyable--not as long as it delivers everything you hoped it would.

Unfortunately, some of those initial dive trips are well remembered for all the wrong reasons, too, since they can easily turn into a disaster if you plan poorly. Too many people believe all you need do is pack your gear to be guaranteed a good time. If that were true, people would never return home disappointed.

Planning a successful dive vacation requires the same care that goes into filing an audit-proof tax return: both demand extensive research and consideration of a wide range of contingencies.

Choosing the right location is critical if you're not to be disappointed. Because of the large number of factors that crop up in making such a decision, it's not as easy as it might seem.

For instance, what kind of diving do you most want to do? What is the one thing you want to see or do on this vacation that you've never experienced before? Are you most interested in photographing or studying marine life, or do you want to prowl the remains of as many shipwrecks as you can? Most places specialize in certain types of activity; there are few that can meet everyone's needs, so you must match your desires with what can realistically be offered.

At large dive resorts, don't expect people to go out of their way to cater to your whims; you'll be only one of many vacationers, and dive operations are geared to satisfying the largest numbers, not the single few.

Here are the major factors to consider:

- PHOTOGRAPHY: If this is your major interest, you'll need to select a spot with good visibility and abundant sea life.

- WRECKS: You're more apt to end up in an area swept by winds and turbulent waters, and where photography will be more difficult.

- SPEARFISHING: If this is foremost on your agenda, you can just about forget foreign travel and plan on staying home. Most good dive destinations ban spearing since the fish life is one of the primary reasons people visit.

- SKILL LEVELS: Do your capabilities match the destination you've chosen? Do all the other accompanying family members also have the experience to dive all the sites a place has to offer? Realistically, there's no sense in choosing a location where you'll frequently encounter currents and be making deep dives if you or a member of your family is still a novice. You won't be comfortable and you won't enjoy it...not unless you intend your 'vacation' to be a combination endurance contest and proving ground. For some reason, most

*Flying to a far-off diving destination doesn't have to be just a fantasy. You can do it.*

women don't appreciate that kind of vacation, and if she's not happy, you won't be either.

- SHORE VS. BOAT DIVING: Do you prefer beach or boat diving? Do you want to spend more time snorkeling than scuba diving? Some sites that are great for scuba are lousy for snorkeling because the reefs start too deep.

- GET SEASICK? If so, avoid places that specialize in long boat trips to the dive sites.

- LAND VS. SEA-SEEING: Do you want to spend your full day diving or only half a day so you can devote time to exploring the land portion of this new part of the world? The options vary at each location, and you need to understand all your options before making a final decision.

- VACATION TIME: How much time do you have for such a vacation? Can you set aside two full weeks so you can visit such legendary and far away places as the

Great Barrier Reef, the Red Sea and the like? Or are you confined to one week--which is only 5 days, really, since two of the 7 are travel days.

Worse yet, are you limited to only a long weekend? If so, you might be surprised at the number of stateside places you could fly or drive to if you timed everything carefully. A dive vacation doesn't have to involve some remote destination to be a memorable one.

● COSTS: Finances are another important problem you must face honestly. Can you really afford to fulfill your dive fantasy? If you think so, are you sure you know all the charges you're likely to encounter? It's surprising how many divers don't anticipate all costs before they depart. For example, are you certain about what the cost of meals will run? In the Caribbean, many hotels routinely charge $20 for dinner, and you may not have anywhere else to dine. A week of such expenses for two--if not anticipated--can be financially disastrous. Plan on spending at least 30% more than your best estimate.

● PACKAGE DEALS: How much do the dives cost? Is it cheaper to buy them as a package in advance or pay on an individual basis? But consider, if you do sign up for a package in advance, you're limited to the services of one dive operation, which prevents you from striking out on your own unless the operator will give you a refund for unused dives. That's yet another point you need to find out in advance, not after you arrive.

● TAXES & TIPS: Are there hotel service charges or special taxes you should know about? Some resorts routinely add a 10-15 percent service charge (tip) as a standard part of the bill. That adds up to a bit of change over an extended period of time. On top of the service charge, there may also be a government tax of an additional 5-10 percent. Combined, these two "extras" can inflate your bill another 25 percent more than what you budgeted for. These are just a few of the financial details you need to research in advance.

*Being able to dive from shore usually allows you to spend more time in the water since you don't have to rely on a boat schedule.*

- KEEPING NON-DIVERS HAPPY: If you're traveling with family members, do they all want to dive as much as you do? If not, what other activities can they become involved in? It's possible there won't be any. It's an old but true adage that the better the diving, the more remote the location. And the more remote the location, the less there is to do but dive. If extensive shopping and an active night life are necessary to keep everyone happy, your diving options become more limited.

- ACCOMMODATIONS: Consider, too, the kind of hotel you want to stay at. Should it be one which is exclusively a dive resort, or would you be happier at a general hotel that offers diving via an arrangement with a dive operation situated off the premises? Do you want to spend your free time with people who have the same interests and who will be happy to swap tales of their own adventures for yours? Then you'll probably have a great time at a dive resort. There is a strong bond, a kind of kinship, among divers that allows for quick friendships on a short vacation.

However, if diving is only one of your reasons for visiting a particular place, you might prefer a more general hotel where you'll have a wider variety of subjects to talk about with other guests at breakfast and dinner. But you might also find it more difficult to make friends because of the greater diversity of interests.

- GROUP VS. SOLO TRAVEL: Would you feel most comfortable if you traveled with a group of people you already knew instead of joining up with a bunch of strangers? If a large dose of familiarity is what you require in an unknown locale, you'll probably feel most comfortable joining a trip offered by the dive shop you frequent at home. That way you know in advance who's going to be present and how compatible the group will be.

- WEATHER: Amazingly, one of the least considered-- yet one of the most crucial--elements of any vacation is the time of year you've chosen. Many people assume that it's warm, sunny and calm in places like Florida and the Caribbean year-round. After all, that's what the travel posters show, right? It's not so. In winter, cold fronts can play havoc with dive schedules as far south as the Caymans. It gets cold, windy, and diving can become disappointing because you can't visit all the sites you want. It's possible the boats might not even be able to go out in extreme situations.

You need to consider carefully the weather patterns: the rainy periods, the hurricane season, the typhoon season, whatever. Nothing ruins a dive trip faster than lousy weather, and though you can't control it, you can minimize its effects according to the time of year you visit a particular locality. Once you've researched this aspect, you could well find you need to switch vacation schedules with a co-worker. That's a lot less aggravating than watching the winds howl while you chalk up expenses of $100-$200 per day sitting in an easy chair.

• TALK TO OTHER DIVERS: Naturally, the best way to learn about a place is talk to someone who's been there. If you're unable to find such a person through your local dive club or dive store, write to the resort and ask them to send some names of previous guests. Then give these former vacationers a call and ask what you need to know. Most people are very helpful as long as your questions are brief and to the point.

Do as much reading as possible before departure in order to become thoroughly familiar with an area. Consult not only dive publications for descriptions of the underwater terrain but invest in general travel guides which will give you detailed points about a place, its people and their customs. The more you know in advance, the more you know what to plan for.

Take all of your own gear except tank and weights, which are normally provided. Rental equipment is not as new or as well maintained as your own. Even if it is, it won't provide the same confidence, or psychological advantage, your own familiar equipment does.

Here's what your equipment list should include: regulator with pressure gauge; mask, fins and snorkel; extra mask and fin straps; buoyancy compensator; wetsuit (which may help you even in the tropics against coral, etc.); knife; dive watch; computer or bottom timer; underwater light for night diving; gloves; decompression tables; a scuba manual for review.

• FIRST AID: After your dive equipment, the most important items you'll need to carry are a variety of remedies for various dive and travel-related ills. For sinus blockage or sticky ears, Sudafeds are widely used since they don't make you drowsy. Also pack some ear wax remover, swimmer's ear medication, sunscreen, Adolph's meat tenderizer for coral scrapes, diarrhea medicine and a simple first aid kit. It's surprising how often you're forced to serve as your own pharmacy because none of the supplies are available.

• TRIP INSURANCE: Before departing, insure your luggage and contents. Your homeowners or tenants policy may already protect you; if not, purchase extra baggage insurance at the airport or through a travel agent. You may also want to purchase trip cancellation insurance to protect you in the event of bad weather, mechanical failure, sickness, etc.

• ELECTRICAL CURRENT: If your vacation is taking you out of the country, ascertain what the electrical current is in the hotels. It may well be 220 volts, which will require a special transformer as well as an adaptor before you can use your rechargeable strobes, hair dryers or any other appliances safely. Those transformers can be purchased only in this country and are available at most electrical supply stores.

• CUSTOMS FORMALITIES: Don't forget to register all your foreign-made items--especially cameras and expensive watches--with U.S. Customs before you depart. Customs has a simple form you must fill out before you leave to avoid paying duty on imported articles when you return. You must show the Customs

*Becoming familiar with overseas diving operations prior to your trip will help avoid unexpected surprises.*

people any equipment you intend to register, so don't pack it away where you can't get to it.

● X-RAYS VS. FILM: Never send your film through airport x-ray machines. One pass may not damage the film, but the effect is cumulative. To avoid any hassle with airport security, put your film in clear plastic canisters, then place these in a double freezer bag. Just hand the bag to the security person, who can scan the visible contents without ever having to open it.

Keep in mind that a diving vacation doesn't need to be reserved just for vacation periods. Whenever you go anywhere, whether for business or pleasure, take along your diving gear and try to go diving.

Not only will you get to enjoy many new places, you'll find it a rewarding experience to meet new people who are just as enthusiastic about diving as you are.

# Chapter 13

## THE ABC'S OF LIVE-ABOARD DIVE VACATIONS

### *How Not to Get Stuck Aboard--or By--a "Flying Dutchman"*

Dive travel is undergoing a revolution. Increasingly each year, the typical dive resort is being bypassed as more people opt to vacation aboard dive cruisers that anchor each day in new spots far from land. Live-aboard diving is the hottest thing since the invention of the B.C.

But, for the unwary and uninformed diver, live-aboard trips offer potential risks. For example, if you check into a dive resort and discover the food is lousy, that the dive personnel are rude and crude and that the compressor isn't working, you can quickly move into another hotel. There aren't many islands with just one dive operation, and there is always safety in numbers.

But once your dive cruiser casts off, you're stuck. There's no turning back. You may hate everything about the place-- your cabin, the crew, the food, the dive sites--but you have to go along for the duration of the cruise. It can turn into a voyage of the damned, especially if you suffer mechanical failure where the compressor breaks down or the engines stop operating.

Some of the live-aboard boats being chartered today are truly floating hotels, boasting air conditioning, total privacy, unlimited hot water and the same spaciousness as a small motel room. Amenities may even surpass most dive resorts by offering a hot tub on the stern and an attentive crew to answer every whim.

Unfortunately, as the number of dive cruisers has proliferated, some old vessels which don't have the space or facilities for extended cruises have been put into service.

What can you do if you're trapped aboard a floating junkpile or if something breaks down on the vacation you took an entire year to save for? What are your legal rights?

Your chances of obtaining a refund or successfully suing the operator depend partly on exactly what went wrong, partly on how you booked your cruise.

According to Barbara Henwood, owner of Europe Travel in Casselberry, FL, for 15 years, the key to a successful dive vacation is to "read before you leave--to know what your rights are so that if you do have a legitimate claim, you can settle it right there at the boat. Don't believe them when they say they'll send you a refund. That's like leaving the scene of an accident without getting the name of the other party's insurance company. The people who get something done are those who won't leave until their complaint is taken care of.

"Remember," she advises, "the boat operator already has all of your money. He can write you a check right there on the spot. Why take his assurances that 'The check will be in the mail.'"

Traveling divers often get themselves into trouble because they don't take the time to read the conditions of their contract, Henwood says. Every tour operator states in their brochure or contract their limits of responsibility and what they will not be held accountable for.

"The problem is no one wants to read all that--they want to have someone tell them what it says," Henwood states. "That's asking for trouble."

Don't hesitate for a moment to demand your rights. You can even quote a little case law: SC 774 which was tried in the District Court of Nassau County, NY. It involved a group of

*Live-aboards aren't dressy and formal like regular cruise ships. This is a last-night costume party.*

irate scuba divers who had purchased a BWIA land-based package "Diving Tour of Tobago."

The divers' complaints were numerous: a delayed flight had cost them their first day of diving, the dive master would not come pick them up at their hotel, dives were canceled-- eventually they made only one of the five dives they had been promised. They grew so disgusted they left the island early and sued the travel agent in small claims court for $1,500, claiming misrepresentation and failure to provide services as promised in the Scuba Tobago brochure. The judge awarded them $685.45

The advice the travel agent gave to his colleagues in an article published in a travel trade magazine: "If you are sued, and it gets to court, PAY THE MONEY (his emphasis)! You are not going to win."

He suggested that agents pay once the suit is filed because not only are they likely to lose anyway, they will also waste an entire day sitting in court.

The law is on your side.

## Weather Problems

Standard exclusions which no one can legally be held accountable for include weather and other acts of God. If you arrive at your boat and find it landlocked because a hurricane is howling your way, you are at the mercy of the dive operator as to whether you obtain a partial refund. The boat must still provide you food and accommodations to fulfill its contract, but whether you get back a portion for the diving depends on the generosity of the boat owner or the travel agency through which you booked.

Or because of the foul weather, you could find yourself diving in a way you never expected--or wanted--in protected waters just off shore, if that's the best the dive operator can do. Legally, every boat has the right to cancel, modify or substitute diving arrangements due to circumstances beyond its control; weather is certainly one of them.

Such a problem is not unique to live-aboard diving. You run the same risk anytime you check into a hotel or dive resort. If the weather is bad and the boats don't go out, you still pay for your room and meals. Unless the diving is paid for as a separate package or on a per-dive basis, you're not apt to get a refund, either.

The best way to protect yourself from getting blown off the water is to check the travel guides about the weather patterns for the part of the world you want to visit. Storms and winds typically are more frequent at some times of the year than at others. If you don't know that, it's your fault.

## Mechanical Failure

Read carefully the liability, responsibility and release agreements that of most dive travel companies have their clients sign. It is enough to make you lose sleep at night.

Specifically, the travel companies normally waive themselves of any responsibility for loss of service as a result of negligence, maintenance, use, operation or control of any of the ships for which they serve as broker. Technically, that means if you sign the waiver and the boat breaks down or

*Live-aboards come in all sizes. Some are large enough to have a fully stocked bar with bartender.*

sinks, that's tough. Dive on it if you want (if you can find some tanks) but that's all you get. That's what the waivers technically say, but do they really mean it? Perhaps not, when it comes to well-established companies like See & Sea, oldest of the dive tour operators, founded in 1966 and since 1972 headed up by well-known photographer Carl Roessler.

Despite what his release says, Roessler freely admits See & Sea has refunded money for missed dives when a boat has had a mechanical problem. "It is impossible to refund for weather--if it's too rough or the sun's not out--but if there is a mechanical failure, we stand behind it," Roessler says. "We have no personal ownership in any of the boats we represent to avoid any conflict of interest, so it's up to us to actively look out for the diver.

"The liability release." Roessler continues, "is to protect ourselves against unreasonable demands from unscrupulous customers who want their money for no valid reason. Some people just enjoy making trouble, for trying to get something

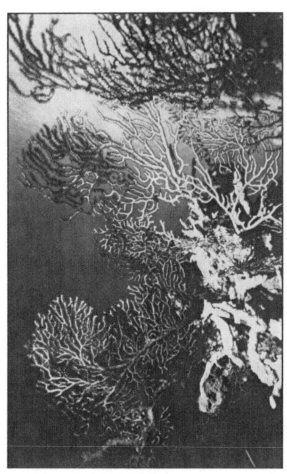

*Live-aboards will always be popular because they take divers to untouched sites where coral growth is most spectacular.*

for nothing, and that's what we're protecting ourselves against."

Roessler says that 95 percent of See & Sea's $4-million a year business is live aboard diving, and that almost half his clients are repeat customers. "I couldn't sell to enough new divers every year to stay in business. The only way to get so many repeats is not to take on a vessel that is not 100 percent. We have to be a Good Housekeeping Seal of Approval. We inspect the boats regularly. A boat can sour fast and do us a lot of word-of-mouth damage quickly. Sometimes a refund is the best investment we can make."

So, with See & Sea and certain other companies, you can be reasonably assured of obtaining a refund when you get back if there's mechanical trouble. However, there are many dive cruisers that take only direct bookings without using an agent. What are your options if there's mechanical failure, even if they've had you sign a waiver? As travel agent Henwood suggests, demand your refund right on the spot. Once you leave, you've lost a great deal of your bargaining power. Despite what a release says, in the U.S. and its territories an operator is expected to provide services as advertised; if he can't because of lousy maintenance or failure to supply a backup compressor (which any dive cruiser should have), he is not likely to convince a judge that he isn't negligent. If the boat has a booking agent back home in the U.S., you can take them to small claims court, which generally has a limit between $1,500 to $2,500. For any amount above that, you'll need to hire a lawyer, and his fees are apt to devour any refund. But making the boat operator as miserable and as unhappy as you are is sometimes incentive enough to pursue a claim.

But, as one attorney advises, in order to file a small claims action you must file it in the city where the agent is doing business. That can pose problems if the booking agent is in New Jersey and you live in Chicago.

The threat of publicity--a nasty letter to "Undercurrent," the "Consumer Reports" of the diving industry--may also prompt a refund if distance prevents you from suing. Bad word-of-mouth and negative publicity can be the kiss of death, and many operators know this. Make them aware that you know it, too, before you leave the ship.

## It's a Scum Bucket!

What if your dive cruiser turns out to be a true scum bucket, something that looks like it was just salvaged from the ocean floor and whose chef is better suited to a garbage truck?

*Don't be gullible enough to simply respond to a beautiful ad in a magazine. Check out every dive operation carefully.*

When things get that bad, you've probably made the biggest mistake of all--not checking on the reputation of the boat, not talking to others who've taken trips aboard her. You wouldn't buy a car without test driving it--why spend several thousand dollars on a vacation without verifying it's exactly what you want and that it works properly?

Before making any boat deposits, ask for the names of 5 or 6 different people in different parts of the country who've made the same cruise within the past 2 or 3 months. Don't go back any farther than this--crews and boats can go downhill amazingly fast. Then phone these people and ask them what you need to know: the quality of diving, equipment used, courteousness of crew, accommodations and food.

Don't be gullible enough to simply respond to a beautiful ad in a magazine. Check it out. Unfortunately, some divers are simply too trusting and believe everything they see advertised. They're the ones who end up on the scum buckets.

If that happens, if you feel you were lied to in the advertisements or during the correspondence with the ship or its booking agent, you can sue for a full refund of the cruise portion of your vacation. We're now dealing with a different area--it's called fraud. However, you cannot normally sue the boat operator for the airfare, since the air carrier supplied its services satisfactorily.

But, as one attorney advised, ask for the airfare as well if you have to hire a lawyer and go to court. Use this argument: you wouldn't have suffered this expense if you hadn't been enticed to do it through the misleading, deceptive advertising. All the court can do is say 'no,' and it might say 'yes.' Obviously, you will need to hire a lawyer in such a case because you are likely to be over the $2,500 small claims court ceiling in most states. Normally, an attorney will be willing to talk over the possibility of a suit with charging a fee for the consultation, then typically will want as much as 30 percent of the amount recovered.

Yet, it may not be possible to file suit if the boat operation is based entirely out of the country. That's why it's so important to get your refund on the spot. But if you booked through a dive shop, you are legally entitled to sue the dive shop instead of the boat owner. The reason is that the shop obviously will have made certain promises and representations about how great the boat is, how superb the diving, in order to collect its commission. The shop is responsible for those claims. Even if you've done business there for years, don't hesitate to sue. The person obviously hasn't done you any favors through his misrepresentation.

### The Ultimate Insurance

The best insurance against a live-aboard disaster is to make yourself informed before investing any money. Ultimately, it's up to you to look out for yourself. That's your best insurance. Even if your legal action is successful or the boat owner refunds your money, the disappointment, aggravation and hassle are likely to outweigh the monetary aspects. And you may become so soured at the idea of live-aboard diving that you'll never try it again, which would be unfortunate.

Still, in case things do go wrong, there are a couple of final safeguards you can employ. One is to pay only by credit card. Don't pay off the balance before you depart; be willing to endure the 18-percent interest for a few months. Then if the engines or compressor do break down or the boat was a reject from some refugee flotilla, write to the credit card company detailing your complaints and refuse to pay. If your complaint is legitimate, most of the time the credit card company will back you, not the boat owner. Unfortunately, not all boats accept credit cards, but many dive shops and travel agencies do.

If you are not dealing with one of the large reputable dive tour companies, it's a good idea to invest in trip cancellation insurance, which can be purchased from any travel agent. Boat operations can--and do--go bankrupt. If they go belly up with your money, you could lose everything; trip cancellation insurance can refund your money. Be sure and read any such policy carefully, because they do differ. Some will refund only if you have medical problems that prevent you from making the trip; the Travelers and other insurance companies also cover operator bankruptcy.

Planning an enjoyable live-aboard vacation takes effort, but considering your financial investment, it's worth doing the extra homework.

*Chapter 14*

THE WORLD'S 10 BEST SCUBA VACATIONS

*You Dive, But Your*
*Significant Other Doesn't*

Because I took up scuba almost 30 years ago when the sport was still in its infancy, I grew accustomed to roughing it on dive trips. Plush dive resorts and comfortable dive boats were nonexistent: I encountered more strange animal life in some lodges than I ever saw on the ocean floor. But that's how dive travel was for many, many years, and I loved it.

When I took a non-diving spouse it didn't occur to me that my new bubble watcher might not share all the same enthusiasm--and tolerance--for some of my favorite dive locations. On our very first trip together we went to Bonaire, where I had a wonderful time photographing the reefs and the profuse marine life. But seven days of sitting by the water and watching goats meander over the barren landscape gave her a severe case of cabin fever, a real strain on both our nerves.

So the next year we went to Bermuda where she could shop, tour museums and be content. Great for her, but lousy for me: the dive boats were landlocked half the time by the wind and Bermuda's wrecks bored me.

Ever since, we've jointly planned our annual jaunts, attempting to find a blend of activities to keep us both happy. Not being a complete fanatic, I quickly appreciated the better service, accommodations and entertainment options she insists upon. It's been a real revelation that on a dive vacation there's something to do at night besides watch algae grow.

In-depth recommendations on dive travel are included in my previous books "Fish & Dive the Caribbean" Vol. 1 and "Fish & Dive Florida & The Keys." For a description and ordering, refer to the Resource Directory at the back of this book.

After a half-dozen years of exploring, I'd recommend the following places for anyone's non-diving family. Although live-aboard dive boats are becoming increasingly popular and the only good way to dive some areas, I've yet to meet anyone's non-diving spouse who didn't instantly mutiny at the idea of being cooped up in tiny quarters with absolutely nothing to do for seven days. Consequently, all these sites are land-based.

## *St. Thomas*

National Geographic Magazine calls Magen's Bay "one of the 10 most beautiful beaches in the world," and, in places, the under water terrain almost matches it. In particular, I like the many options--reefs, wrecks and open ocean diving. Few places offer all three in such comfortable surroundings. On shallow reefs only 40 to 80 feet, typically I've found big rays, octopus and loads of fish. However, my favorite photo stops are the many stone tunnels which, like Bonaire's fabulous pier pilings, are covered with encrusting sponges, tubastrea corals, crabs and shrimps. I always reserve at least one night out in the shallows at Cow and Calf, often spectacular for macro pictures. The deep dives in open ocean 4-6 miles offshore feature large pelagic species and turtles. I never miss an easy day-trip to the British Virgins to dive the famed wreck of the "Rhone," filming location for "The Deep."

For the beach bound, St. Thomas is a shopper's paradise. In the capital of Charlotte Amalie, over 100 shops stock the finest clothing, European crystal and china, jewelry, Swiss watches and French perfumes, all at bargain prices thanks to

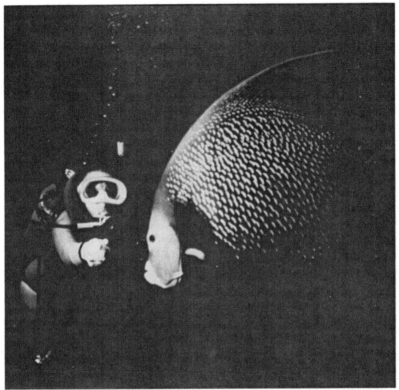

*Night diving is a common feature at the world's best diving sites.*

St. Thomas' freeport status. Further, some of the Caribbean's most exclusive resorts are found on St. Thomas, all within a short drive of the many dive operators. Barring a hurricane, weather is normally good year-round. But beware of flying in through San Juan on any of the small local airlines. They are notorious for being late and extremely sloppy with baggage. It's taken as long as two days for my gear to arrive, one parcel at a time. I refuse anything but a direct flight into Harry S. Truman Airport aboard a major carrier. For information, contact U.S. Virgin Islands Tourist Information Office, 1270 Ave.of the Americas, New York, NY 10020; 212-582-4520.

## Grand Cayman

Skin Diver Magazine once dubbed Grand Cayman the "Super Bowl of Scuba," and that about sums it up. Cayman's famed North Wall well deserves its unquestioned rating as one of the most spectacular dives in the Caribbean. Huge purple sea fans, bright red finger sponges and colorful corals cluster near the top between 60-90 feet. I always visit the big school of 20-lb tarpon that stays permanently in one valley, though tame marine life abounds on all the reefs and wrecks. Grand Cayman is also the submarine capital of the world: two four-man Research Submersible Ltd. (RSL) subs serve as space shuttles in reverse, carrying passengers to an incredible 800 feet, while a specially-built tourist sub "Atlantis" ferries groups of 28 down to 130 feet. I've done both, but nothing can match the RSL experience since it visits where no scuba diver can ever go.

Audie Murphy isn't the only one who can go to Hell and back; the whole family can, too, as part of a general island tour. Hell is actually a weird-looking volcanic rock formation near the giant turtle farm (open to visitors). Also available is the Jack Nicklaus-designed Britannia golf course offering nine holes of Cayman golf, which features a golf ball that only travels half as far as a regular golf ball (this is a small island after all). For watersports, nothing tops the Holiday Inn on beautiful 7-mile beach, with parasailing, jet skis, sailboats and picnic cruises. My bubble watcher reports shopping in the capital of George Town is worth perhaps half a day, but except for local crafts the variety is limited.

Diving is most reliable in summer, though even then wind can sometimes knock out trips to the North Wall for 2-3 days at a time. Contact Cayman Islands Dept. of Tourism, 250 Catalonia Ave., Coral Gables, FL 33134; 305-444-6551.

## Cozumel

Cozumel owes much of its fame to its clear water. On a bad day the visibility is only 100 feet. Sometimes it's an incredibly clear 250 feet, almost as good as seeing on land.

The diving reflects Cozumel's strong Mexican flavor through its fleet of motor-sailors that make full-day trips with

*On Grand Cayman, going to Hell, and leaving it, is no big deal. This is one of Hell's gift shops.*

a lunch of fresh-cooked seafood over an open beach fire. The morning dive, a drift in strong current, demands continued attention as divers glide along the bottom and just over the reefs. It's my favorite method for seeing a lot of territory quickly--and the only sane way since it's impossible to combat the current. Afternoons are spent in locations where current is absent.

Compared to most Caribbean islands, Cozumel has a refreshing charm. Once part of the vast Maya empire, land tours to several primitive island ruins are offered, but the best bet is to take a tour into the heart of the Yucatan to visit the more impressive sites at Chichen Itza, Uxmal, Tulum and Coba. Plenty of local beaches to drive to, and if shopping in the only town of San Miguel proves unsatisfactory, it's easy to hop a plane to nearby Cancun. I've always enjoyed dining in Cozumel since the cuisine is still authentic and not the corrupted Tex-Mex. Seafood is also popular, especially lobster. The best hotels are clustered at the northern end of the beach. Most offer evening entertainment, and a few have moon-lit cruises. Dive boats pick you up at your hotel.

Weather is most reliable in summer, when it's also hottest, but whenever you visit, remember this is also the land of mañana. And be sure and pack the doxycycline or Lomotil; otherwise, Montezuma's revenge may closet you temporarily. Contact Tourist Information Center, Cozumel, Quintana Roo, Mexico; telephone 2-09-72.

## Florida Keys

One of the few places you can drive right to the dive boat from your home, the Keys are the most dived location in the entire U.S., particularly the John Pennekamp Coral Reef State Park at Key Largo. With so many divers (over 500,000 annually), dive operators often look beyond the standard C cards to gauge experience level. I always bring a logbook in order to avoid the typical 20- 40-foot two-tank dives and instead sign up for all-day safaris to deeper, less crowded regions.

Like most advanced divers, I try as much as possible to bypass the crowds in Pennekamp (birthplace of cattle-car dive boats) though first timers should see the Christ of the Deep statue or famed Molasses Reef with its colorful coral and massive schools of grunt and snapper. I prefer Marathon/ Big Pine Key in the Middle Keys, site of Looe Key, one of Florida's most beautiful, varied and prolific reefs. Or, Key West, where relatively few divers ever take the trouble to go. Key West, about a hundred miles below Key Largo, unquestionably is the most interesting city in the Keys and the diving is about as good here as else where--just fewer people.

A good week's itinerary would allow for a full day each at Pennekamp and the Middle Keys, with the rest of the week in Key West. Key West hotels, restaurants and many interesting sights (Hemingway's house, Audubon house) make the other areas seem like small backwater burgs (which they are).

I've never had good luck diving the Keys in winter; I always seem to arrive along with a cold front, which keeps the boats docked. Spring, summer and fall are safest but never come during a holiday period. It would be hard to see the marine life for all the flippers. Contact: Florida Keys Tourism, P.O. Box 1147, Key West, FL 33040;800-FLA-KEYS.

*It helps if your destination has good snorkeling so you can spend quality water time with your non-diving partner.*

## North Channel Islands

California's towering kelp forests are the marine equivalents of giant redwoods, except they contain considerably more wildlife--sea lions, seals, huge schools of fish sometimes so thick it's been hard to locate my partner. Caribbean reefs can seem remarkably bare compared to these kelp wonderlands. Although the kelp has been hurt in some areas, it's still

*123*

strong, healthy and thick at the North Channel Islands of San Miguel, Santa Rosa, Santa Cruz and Anacapa, which can be dived from Santa Barbara or Ventura. These islands, actually a seaward extension of the Santa Monica mountains, are one of the few places divers are still allowed to hunt fish, subject to the regulations of the Channel Islands National Park and the Dept. of Game and Fish. My one complaint is the year-round cold water that demands a full wet suit, hood and gloves. Water temps are in the 50's in winter, the 60's in summer.

Santa Barbara is about two hours driving time above Los Angeles, so the shopping prospects are endless. Santa Barbara, in the foothills of the Los Padres National Forest, is noted for its Spanish architecture, immaculate look and monied residents. Hotel and restaurant selection are superb: a true luxury vacation with none of the hassles of international travel. Weather is a potential problem in spring. Contact: Truth Aquatics Inc., Sea Landing Breakwater, Santa Barbara, CA 93109; 805-963-3564.

## *Great Barrier Reef*

Compared to many places, the visibility at Heron Island (Australia's best Great Barrier Reef resort) is downright poor. Sometimes it's only 20 feet and its best clears only to 70. But clear water is easy to find and not nearly as important as the big bright soft corals, nudibranchs, starfish and Tridachna clams as well as big batfish, barracuda, wobbegong sharks, coral trout and sweetlips that command attention here. Twice daily trips choose from 16 different sites 50 miles off the Queensland coast with depths ranging between 30-70 feet. The bommies (coral heads) are famous for their tame fish. I'm particularly fond of the big batfish there that school right up to a camera lens.

Heron Island itself is a Marine National Park, so all fish, corals and birdlife are protected. As Heron is only a third of a mile long and 300 yards wide, I'm fortunate my non-diving spouse is a nature lover. While I photographed fish, she counted birds. An estimated 90,000 noddy terns live at Heron year-round, and another 17,000 mutton birds visit seasonally.

*Heron Island on Australia's Great Barrier Reef, long a world-class diving center. The helicopter approach is an unforgettable experience.*

At low tide, she joined a guided reef walk in the shallows (sneakers mandatory) where tropicals and many other species remain trapped until the water level rises. At night, we both watched green and logger head turtles deposit eggs on the beach (Nov.-March only). Being below the equator, best weather often is during our winter. The helicopter trip from Gladstone to Heron is far better than the boat ride because it orients you to the reef system and offers great aerial photography. Contact: P&O Resort Holidays, 800/225-9849 for both U.S. and Canada.

## Advanced Travel

These next islands are for those who've already made quite a few dive vacations and yearn for something really different. Most of these places are quite a bit of trouble to get to, and landbased activities may be even more limited than at Heron Island.

# *Truk*

Located in Micronesia, during WW II this magnificent 822-square-mile lagoon sheltered the formidable Japanese Imperial Fleet at the largest naval base outside Japan. In a single surprise bombing attack, U.S. forces sunk 60 of Japan's finest floating fortresses, including the "Fujikawa Maru" and the "Shinkoko Maru."
Today, the ships share the bottom with another 40 wrecks including aircraft, making this the finest wreck diving grounds in the world, a rare wonderful opportunity to see so many intact wrecks so close together. Most are slowly evolving into massive coral gardens. Since many of the best dives are below 80 feet, I'd advise this trip only for the properly experienced. The single hotel is the adequate but unspectacular 100-room, air-conditioned Truk Continental. Out side of a land tour and a lagoon cruise, other activities are limited. Contact Poseidon Ventures Dive Tours, 359 San Miguel Dr., Newport Beach, CA 92660; 800-854-9334.

## *New Guinea*

Papua is a God-send for those of us forced to give up live-aboard boats. Papua's diving is considered as good as any in the Pacific, but it's one of the few places to enjoy all the wonderfully exotic marine life while still remaining land-based. Stay at Jais Aben resort on the north shore at Madang: I was amazed that just 15 yards offshore I suddenly found myself over a steep wall plummeting hundreds of feet. Caves, crinoids, big sea fans, soft corals and even the wreck of a WW II B-25 Mitchell bomber all are within a 10-minute boat ride.
I dove here almost non-stop: at night, macro photography at the Jais Aben dock is superb. If WW II remains are a special interest, try nearby Rabul island and the Kaivuna Hotel. They'll find you at least 10 plane and ship wrecks.
Shopping for native handicrafts and the opportunity to view a culture moving from very primitive stages directly into the computer age are the main shore activities. It's well worthwhile to spend a few days in the highlands to view the colorful native dress and a land still largely untouched by

modern man. Contact: Sea Safaris, 3770 Highland Ave., Manhattan Beach, CA 90266; 213-546-2464.

## Seychelles

These tiny islands in the Indian Ocean are so stunning that early European explorers thought they were surviving fragments of the original Garden of Eden. Most divers would also agree. Diving is centered at Mahe, the Seychelles' economic and political center. Mahe alone boasts 68 beaches and waters teeming with a mind-boggling 900 species of fish and 600 species of coral! I still find the diversity of marine life difficult to comprehend.

Hiking tours of the rain forest, a visit to a working tea plantation, craft shops, art galleries and a colorful fruit and vegetable garden in the city of Victoria were as much fun as the diving. We also spent a non-diving day on nearby Praslin island, home of the unique Coco-de-Mer palm in the breathtakingly beautiful Vallee de Mai. Good hotels on Mahe are the Coral Strand (also the diving hq.), Sunset Beach and Fisher man's Cove. Avoid the rainy season Dec.-Jan. Contact: Sea Safaris (see New Guinea listing), Travel Seychelles (813/ 387-0027) or Seychelles Tourist Board, 820 Second Ave., Suite 900F, New York, NY 10017; 212/687-9766.

But as much as I've enjoyed these many places, next trip I want to go back to the spot that caused all this research, balmy Bonaire in the Netherlands Antilles. They now have two casinos, improved fishing facilities, birdwatching, caving, horseback riding, evening slide shows and tours of the national park. Not bad for my favorite desert island, surrounded by an oasis of reefs. In my book, it's always been a Top 10.

*Chapter 15*

*THE WORLD'S 10 BEST SNORKELING SITES*

*Where You Don't Have to Scuba To Have the Front Row Advantage*

In this high-tech era of wrist computers and mixed gas, it's easy to forget snorkeling still survives as the heart of the sport. Nothing allows more freedom of movement or the same exhilarating feeling of oneness with your environment than simply floating on water.

Snorkelers need only take a single step over the transom to propel themselves into an alternative world, a realm where the residents are far more colorful and lively than on land. No wonder snorkeling was originally known as "free diving."

So it's quite understandable that thousands more people don mask, fins and snorkel each year than air tanks. What they see often equals, if not surpasses, what scuba divers encounter.

Naming the world's 10 best snorkeling spots is as difficult as deciding who has the world's best cuisine. Some people prefer spicy salsa, others yearn for thick creamy sauces.

The following consensus is based on over 30 years of personal experience plus interviews with some of the country's top underwater guides, writers, photographers, and dive travel company operators. The opportunity to interact with marine life, not just sightsee, was an important criteria in making the Top 10 list.

This "best of the best," not listed in any particular order, is a revealing reflection of the amazing diversity you can enjoy in the shallows world-wide. Since many of these places have equally good scuba diving, they are ideal vacations to propose to a non-diving spouse or a friend. What better way to motivate them to evolve from snorkeler to qualified diver?

## *Crystal River, Florida*

Snorkeling the springs in Kings Bay at the headwaters of Crystal River is a bit like floating through a series of ether-clear limestone aquariums. Here, cool waters from deep inside the state aquifer surge up through 30 known springheads in the bay, spread generously out, and then reconverge and run off into the bucolic Crystal River and the Gulf of Mexico. Many of the springs hide small caves, like King's Spring, which drops from four feet of water to 30 just off the south bank of Banana Island, forming spectacular rocky cliffs and crevices in the soft rock below.

Giant tarpon visit here, along with salt water snapper, freshwater bream, largemouth bass and jack crevalle. If that's not variety enough, you're also likely to see one of the 2,000-pound West Indian Manatees that winter here in the 72-degree water. Crystal River is the only place in the world you can swim face-to-face in vodka-clear water with this gentle and giant herbivore.

Manatees, the apparent basis for the mermaid legend, are a composite of land and sea animal grafted together in a distant time; in fact, their closest living relative is the elephant. Manatees are protected by law from harassment, but many of these gentle giants actively seek out human company.

## *North Shore, Providenciales*

The clear, amazingly colorful and fish-filled patch reefs inside the barrier reef bordering Provo's north shore are like bonsai gardens, miniature fans, corals and sponges sculpted

*Snorkelers have as many exotic destinations to choose from as divers.*

and neatly arranged over terrain alternating between hilly and flat. Many coral fans there are a brilliant yellow and light tan instead of plain royal purple. The patch reefs begin right offshore, the same ideal situation that made Bonaire so famous. Only Provo's corals are considerably healthier, unaffected by intense development, effluent runoff or heavy snorkeler traffic.

Provo's patch reefs sit on a shallow shelf surrounded by deep water, an arrangement that provides snorkelers a glimpse of marine animals who usually cruise at far greater depths. For example, you may sometimes spot marine turtles resting on the bottom, other times lazily swimming by. Or confront the familiar torpedo shapes of nurse and blackfin sharks at close range . Perhaps most surprising of all, you may even encounter a large 3-4 pound lobster out Bogart-ing around for a stroll in the middle of the day. And to think Provo, most famous of the landfalls in the Turks & Caicos chain, is best known for its deep water diving!

## Heron Island, Australia

Strung out like row after row of khaki, purple or green colored frisbees, the plate corals adjacent to Heron Island have the same characteristic toe-sized protruding nodules. This healthy fringing reef harbors a volume and variety of marine that is truly amazing.

Small clams, their blue-green fleshy mantles open and visible, encrust to the coral in many places. At low tide, when as much as 12 miles of reefline is exposed, the sound of the clams squirting water is the only sound to break the stillness.

Large black and maroon sea cucumbers lay in the sand adjacent to or under the coral; their long twisting shapes appear like carelessly flung lumps of salt water taffy. However, the most impressive creatures are the large cobalt blue starfish, similar in size and shape to the ornaments placed atop Christmas trees.

At low tide, a marine park naturalist will walk with you among the shallows to explain the types of corals and fish that flourish there. At high tide, when the water has risen 10-15 feet, you return and snorkel at the same spot or swim out straight out for several hundred yards in any direction. The waters surrounding Heron have been a protected marine sanctuary for decades, so the marine life is always at peak condition.

Located about 50 miles from the mainland, Heron Island is a small 42-acre coral cay. But one of approximately 900 islands located among the more than 2,600 individual reefs that comprise the greatest living organism on earth, the 1200-mile long Great Barrier Reef, it is a microcosm of the Great Barrier Reef at its best.

At high tide, Heron Island's coral plateau is rich in nudibranchs, the tiny, delicately colored snails that live without shells. You may never again witness such a variety in a single spot. Turtles also come ashore to nest from October to March, another sight common then in the shallows.

## Sting Ray City, Grand Cayman

Watching the curved, smiling mouth of a southern sting ray as it turns on its back and glides by next to you is always a

*Many good snorkel sites have reefs close to shore so they can be enjoyed any time of day or night.*

memorable sight. But it doesn't begin to compare to suddenly noticing a ray is gliding between your legs, or to feeling another one inching up the length of your torso, its silky smooth underbody pressed next to you. Talk about sensory overload!

But the southern sting rays of Grand Cayman, concentrated in a school of 15 to 20 animals in a 10-foot deep section of the protected North Sound, enjoy contact with people. And although the rays still possess that dreaded tail stinger for which they are so noted, no one has ever been injured in the years man and rays have hobnobbed together. So, to date, it's been safe even to allow children to watch all the wing flapping from the same bird's eye view.

The sting rays, however, are inclined to stay near the bottom. You have to bring food to entice them near the surface and create the same kind of melee created by divers (who also use food as an attractor). That's about as difficult to achieve as getting that "piranha of the ocean," the yellowtail snapper, to eat out of your hand; only the rays are better mannered.

The North Sound's bright sand bottom acts as a giant reflector, making this one of the best photo opportunities available to snorkelers anywhere. Where else can you get sting rays to come so close to your face they're sometimes out of focus?

## Gulf of Aqaba, Red Sea

Imagine how the cement side of a swimming pool edges right up to the soil. Transform that top cement layer to a living reef that grows right next to shore, then drops off sharply just like the side of a pool. Now you have the same unique conditions that exist at the mouth of the Gulf of Aqaba, where, not one, but three reefs contain all the breathtakingly colorful corals for which the Red Sea is so famous.

The approach is down an easy hill incline. The reefs, known as the Far and Near Gardens and Ras Um Sid, begin in only about a foot and a half of water. It's an eerie snorkeling experience, as if you were swimming over the top of a deep wall that suddenly plummets into water seemingly as deep as

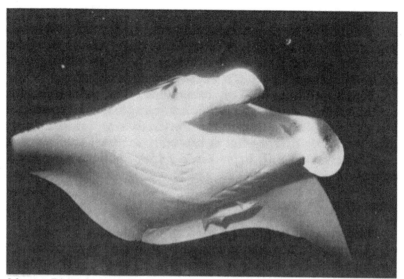

*Manta Ridge on the Pacific Island of Yap provides good views to snorkelers as well as divers.*

the Cayman Trench. On one side of you is the coral reef...on the other, nothing but deep dropoff blue. That is a sight few snorkelers ever get to experience, anywhere.

The mouth of the Gulf of Aqaba is also one of the few places snorkelers can savor some of the truly emblematic Red Sea marine life, like the bump-head wrasse or the big fluffy soft corals that resemble overstuffed pillows. Such deep water creatures, normally denied snorkelers, display themselves prominently here.

## *Qamea, Fiji*

Not only do the mind-blowing, billowing soft red corals Fiji is famed for thrive right offshore at Qamea, but also formations in vibrant yellows, oranges and pinks. These soft corals flourish best in nutrient rich, fast flowing water, and the channel separating Qamea (pronounced Guh-may-ah) from Taveuni, just 3 miles west, provides the perfect conditions for optimum growth. Needless to say, fish are fond of this area as well. In addition to Qamea, excellent snorkeling is possible both at Taveuni and nearby Matagi.

Depending on where you explore, the currents so vital for the distinctive coral gardens could also require drift snorkeling or precise water entry timing to correspond with the tidal flow. To witness what many consider The True World Exposition of soft corals--that's worth any extra effort.

The South Seas idyll of deserted beaches, palm tree sunsets and friendly islanders is quickly fading as Fiji becomes the hottest dive destination in the Pacific Basin. Qamea, however, not only offers what is probably the best shallow soft coral sites in all Fiji, it provides a rare idyllic setting for a complete getaway.

## Madang, Papua, New Guinea

The sign of a healthy reef is the amount of noise it produces. A robust reef is a racket-producing place of crackling and popping sounds as reef residents go about their daily tasks. The reefs near Madang are so untouched that when you put your head in the water, the clamor is like a Geiger counter reading the meltdown at Chernobyl. The soft corals are almost as much of a visual shock; their colors may make you wonder when all the Caribbean reefs were bleached out the next time you visit there.

Armor-spiked lionfish, the underwater version of the porcupine, are highly-sought photographic subjects, as are long-dorsaled Moorish idols and the ever-popular clownfish. You'll usually locate the orange-colored clownfish, laced with melting vanilla ice cream markings, at home in or near a large anenome.

Madang, often called the "Prettiest Town in the South Pacific," and PNG's most tourist-oriented area, provides the most accessible snorkeling. But go to PNG only when you have the time truly to concentrate and appreciate both the sea and land that surround you. Everything about Papua New Guinea demands your complete attention. Both the sea life thriving in the warm waters and the near stone-age cultures residing in the mountainous rainforests will strongly compete for your attention. It's as if sea and land decided to see which could most successfully vie for a traveler's attention. It's clearly a tie; they both win.

## Yap, Micronesia

Hanging at the end of a line as the current swirls around you, a huge bat-like apparition that seems the size of several large garage doors approaches from the depths. Another creature follows, and another and another...all coming in your direction. Moments later, these huge titans as much as 12-feet across pause directly beneath you. These are the spectacular but harmless giant rays at Manta Ridge on the island of Yap, in Micronesia, between Palau and Guam.

Observing a single manta ray up close is a rare occurrence. To be able to anticipate when a group of what the Mexicans term "devil fish" will appear almost on a time schedule according to tide is astounding. The mantas choose this particular section of the 100-foot wide channel because of the small tropical fish that live on a ridge crest at 30 feet. The tiny yellow and blue fish dart about the mantas' bodies and gills to pick away parasites, nature's model of an efficient cleaning station. The mantas of Yap don't need to jump on the surface to dislodge parasites as mantas normally do, only suspend over this ridge to let the cleaner fish do their work.

How reliable are the mantas? Manta Ray Bay Hotel guarantees them: no rays, no pay. You'll be out only the price of your plane ticket and what you eat and drink. Considering all the exaggerated claims in diving and snorkeling, that's as good as it gets.

## Delos, Greece

It doesn't seem possible that anything could survive underwater for more than 2,000 years. Yet on the bottom scant feet below you is a scene from the discovery of Atlantis: sunken temple columns, amphorae and still recognizable pieces of mosaic scattered all over the bottom. This scene is real, not fantasy, and the artifacts are enduring fragments from the Golden Age of Greece. These 15- to 25-foot shallows encircling the Greek isle of Delos, one of the great archaeological wonders of the ancient world, are a special snorkelers' preserve.

Although Delos was the treasury of the Athenian empire as far back as 478 B.C. and also served as the commercial center of the Aegean, the tiny island was a sacred sanctuary where it was forbidden for any mere mortal to die or be born. According to legend, the island drifted beneath the waves of the Aegean until the god Poseidon (Neptune) himself raised this rugged mass of granite from the sea as the birthplace for Apollo, the sun god, and his twin sister Artemis, goddess of the moon.

At one time, even the Hollywood version of the intact sunken temple may have existed here. Unfortunately, museum scavenging by many different nations has removed literally tons of objects from the water.

Today, all that exists on Delos today are archaeological remains, including the sacred temples to Apollo and Artemis; and mosaics, some featuring the likeness of dolphins which still roam these waters. Greece, anxious to protect its remaining heritage, forbids scuba diving anywhere in its territorial waters. Which is why only snorkelers have the privilege of drifting above this birthplace of the ancient gods.

## La Paz, Mexico

A grinning sea lion bobs up inches from your face, squaring off eye-to-eye. It playfully lunges for your snorkel just as another animal nips your fins. In the immortal words of Cindy Lauper, these critters "just want to have fun."

The sea lion colony at Los Islotes in southern Baja is always eager to jump in and play. And the animals don't even expect to be fed, probably because this protected bay in the Sea of Cortez is usually loaded with sardines. It's shallow enough around the rocky promontory, only 10-15 deep, that you can keep up with every bit of frenetic activity taking place in the water.

A snorkel with sea lions can be a non-stop session of water aerobics. After an hour of thrashing around and almost-continuous bumping body contact, you may well emerge from the water fairly exhausted; but certainly happy.

By then, sounds of the excited, barking sea lions will have you wishing for ear plugs. As everyone who's ever attended a circus knows, a single performing sea lion is noisy enough. Amplify that by a hundred voices, and you begin to get an idea of the constant din that surrounds snorkelers at the sea lion rookery of Los Islotes. This is one of the few times when hearing is as meaningful as seeing.

## How To Get There

Among the many dive travel operators, Sea Safaris specializes in arranging trips geared especially toward pleasing snorkelers. They are familiar with most of the sites on our Top 10 list. Call toll free 800/821-6670 nationwide/Canada or 800/262-6670 in California.

CRYSTAL RIVER: As many as 50 more manatees will winter at Crystal River between November and March. Small john boats with outboards can be rented at several marinas near King's Spring. Contact the Citrus County Chamber of Commerce, City/County Bldg., Crystal River, FL 32629; 904/795-3149.

HERON ISLAND, AUSTRALIA: April through July is the best snorkel season. The resort covers about one-third of the 42-acre island. The rest is a natural preserve and a rookery for terns and herons. Contact P&O Resorts, Ltd., 800/225-9849 (US/Canada) or 408/685-8902.

PROVO, TURKS & CAICOS: Best diving definitely is in summer. Wind can be a real problem during winter. Contact the Turquoise Reef Resort & Dive Provo: 800/234-PROVO.

STING RAY CITY, GRAND CAYMAN: The protected waters of the North Sound can be dived anytime of year, although the water can turn greenish in summer. Contact Cayman Islands Dept. of Tourism, 250 Catalonia Ave., Coral Gables, FL 33134; 305/444-651.

GULF OF AQABA, RED SEA: You need a local guide and a jeep to find our Top 10 site. August and September are heat-stroke hot. Winds in January sometimes are a problem.

QAMEA, FIJI: Wettest months are from the end of January to the beginning of April. The reef is close to shore at one end of the 43-acre island. The island's single hotel with complete facilities has only 10 waterfront lodgings known as "bures." Fiji Visitor's Bureau, tel. 213/568-1616; fax 213/670-2318. Qamea Beach Club, phone/fax 679/880-220.

MADANG, PAPUA NEW GUINEA: Avoid the month of January when rains are hard and heavy, like the precursor to the next Great Flood. Some resorts even close then. Official wet season is from the end of November to April; outside January, rain tends to be brief though hard but usually don't affect visibility. Contact Sea Safaris (800/821-6670); Adventure Express, 800/443-0799; or Tropical Adventures, 800/247-3483.

YAP, MICRONESIA: Although the mantas do move according to the season, observing them is guaranteed any time of year. Like most guarantees, it is limited: that you will see mantas at least once if you stay five nights, snorkel for 4 days. The strongest currents are around the full moon and could give you the ride of your life. Wettest months are July and August. Contact the Manta Ray Bay Hotel & Yap Divers, P.O. Box 177, Yap, FSM 96943; tel. 011-691-350-2300/1/2; or fax 011-691-350-4110.

DELOS, GREECE: Summer is best although you want to avoid around Aug. 15, the time of the meltemi (etesian wind) when seas can turn rough; not always enough interest for trips the rest of the year. No facilities on the island; must be dived by a boat coming over from Mykonos, only 2 miles away. Because of the ban on scuba diving, most U.S. dive tour operators do not conduct trips; see your local travel agent.

LA PAZ, MEXICO: Best snorkeling conditions are from June to November when water temps vary between 75 and 85 degrees and visibility may be as much as 100 feet. Winter winds and plankton blooms November through March when 20-30 feet is average. Contact Baja Diving & La Concha Beach Resort in La Paz through Sea Safaris.

# Chapter 16

## TRAVEL TIPS FOR THE TROPICS

### Adapting to New Conditions Is Essential

Most of the world's best diving occurs in tropical or semitropical waters. A few advance preparations, both mentally and physically, will help ensure a good time.

### The Time Warp

You enter a strange time dimension once you land on a tropical island. Time may seem to stand still or even run backwards. Things just don't happen as quickly or as precisely as you may be accustomed to. This characteristic varies enough from island to island that each seems to have its own unique set of clocks. It drives some visitors crazy.

In Mexico, it's known as the difference between "Mexican time" and "gringo time." In the tropics, it's simply known as "island time," as opposed to real time.

It can be frustrating, no doubt about it. After rushing to put things in order at work, dashing around to shop and then pack, and hurrying to the airport, many visitors arrive on island still stuck in warp drive. Some quickly get upset when islanders don't share the same sense of urgency. Others become infuriated that locals won't respond as promptly and as efficiently to every request as employees or service personnel do back home.

There are two ways to deal with the situation...you can either adapt to it, or fight it. Yes, your visit is on a time budget. You want to fit in as much as you can--but you also want to enjoy every activity as much as possible. It's the old "quantity time vs. quality time" issue. The setting has just changed, that's all.

One way to decompress from Western-style living almost immediately is to do nothing the day of your arrival except have something to drink, eat, look around a little and go to sleep early. You'll wake up in a more relaxed mood the next morning. If you arrive tired and stay tired--the repeated diving will probably wear you out eventually, anyway--your vacation may turn into nothing but an ordeal.

So don't schedule anything important your first full day on island except for the diving. Between periods, just laze around and get to know the place. Find out what the time flow is and go with it. What are the things you really want to do and see? Do things usually start 10 minutes late? Or is the average closer to 30 minutes? Or maybe--and this does happen at well-managed properties--real time is the norm.

Dive operators usually keep to the clock. They have to in order to get their boats in and out on time. The rest of the hotel staff, however, may be doing its own thing...individually.

The amazing thing is that if you don't try and fight the system, everything eventually gets done. Perhaps not in the way or manner you expect, but it eventually happens. Visitors to Jamaica, after their first few days of getting acclimated to the usual delays, quickly adopt the phrase "No problem, mon" as part of their standard vocabulary.

If you're on-island for a week or two, you gradually begin to realize that many of the things you typically feel anxious about are nothing but artificial pressures created by our own culture. Accustomed to knowing the latest news and current events almost as they happen? Before long, you realize that what's happening thousands of miles away is not all that important. You're not part of it. You can't affect it. So why worry or be concerned about it? Going from deadline to

*Trying new foods is part of the fun in traveling to the tropics.*

deadline is merely one way to live...not necessarily the only
way and certainly not the best.

Of course you can try and fight the system. That doesn't
work much better in the Caribbean than it does back home.
Islanders are used to impatient tourists. What you have to say
won't be anything they haven't heard before. And, don't ever
forget, they are in the position to retaliate.

Some visitors never do adapt to the concept of island time. They usually don't go back. There is a difference, however, between poor, sloppy service and doing things at a different tempo. Definitely complain about any poor, sloppy service.

## The Bugs

The worst are usually not mosquitoes but the no-see-ums, also called midges and sand flies, usually concentrated on beaches around sunrise and sunset. They are so tiny as to be invisible, but what exists must be all teeth. In Spanish, they are known as mi-mis (pronounced "me-mees" as in "a case of the screaming mee-mees!"). Long pants and shoes/socks are the best protection.

- **Repellent:** Avon's "Skin So Soft" is not only effective, it doesn't have the industrial chemical odor of most strong commercial repellents. Pour the "Skin So Soft" into a pump aerosol and liberally spray your ankles and waist to repel ticks and mites. Also spray your clothes. Otherwise, rely on chemical preparations with Deet. At least, when using "Skin So Soft," you will smell sweet--not sour--which makes it easier to mingle with the locals. At the same time, avoid sweet-smelling soaps, perfumes and colognes, which attract insects better than they do the opposite sex.

- **Bites:** Baking soda solutions help relieve itching. Papaya, the main ingredient in Adolph's meat tenderizer, is a native of the Caribbean. It's a good pain killer for nonpoisonous stings (fire coral scrapes, too). The papaya enzyme breaks down the insect venom so it no longer stings. Regular antihistamine tablets taken for allergies or colds also help reduce swelling and itching; antihistamine in cream form may cause skin allergies. Cortisone cream also helps stop itching, rashes. One way to reduce bites: always wear socks.

- **Vitamin Supplements:** Ever notice how some people get eaten alive by insects while others just stand around and watch? Body chemistry appears to contribute to

144

this. Vitamin B-1 supplements and odorless garlic capsules do seem to work as natural insect repellents for some people.

## Staying Healthy

● **Colds & Allergies:** Colds are not normally the problem. Allergies are. Many divers suffer an allergic reaction to a plant they may have never encountered before. With hundreds of species of trees, flowers and orchids in the tropics, something is always in bloom, always dropping pollen. Take non-drowsy antihistamines to plug the sniffles and teary eyes during the day. At night, don't worry about something that may knock you out. Take whatever works best and get some sleep.

● **High Humidity & Dehydration:** You'll lose a lot of liquid sweating. Not replacing it will make you feel tired and lousy. Drink liquids before you feel thirsty. If you wait until your mouth feels dry, you've waited too long too late. Drink plenty of liquid at night and at breakfast to get you through each day. It takes about two weeks to adjust to high humidity, but you can keep your energy level up by doing some of the following:

1) Air conditioning: if you're accustomed to it at home, sleep with it on at night. You will feel far more rested than if you'd slept with a ceiling fan and a natural breeze; you're making a lot of high energy demands on your body during the day, so pamper it at night.

2) Salt: while generally something to avoid, you need to increase your intake in the tropics to conserve body fluid.

3) Potassium/rehydration salt supplements: if you still feel drained and can't kick into gear, try these in moderation. Eat several bananas every morning. They are rich in potassium (so is ketchup, for that matter).

4) Alcohol and colas: avoid both as much as possible. Both are diuretics, which will drain you even more. Dehydration is one of the most common causes of the bends. You can get bent even if you follow the tables conservatively when you're dehydrated. Drink fresh juices instead.

- **Intestinal Problems:** Usually the result of a bacterial infection or consuming strange food and drink (beware those rum punches). In some remote regions, tap water may be unsafe during the rainy season. Diarrhea and dehydration are the most serious problems: drink plenty of fluids except alcohol and milk, which seem to prolong bouts of diarrhea. A bland diet of tea and toast seems to help some people. Although it usually clears up on its own after a couple of days, medication can control attacks almost immediately. Use loperamide (brand name, Imodium) and atropine (Lomotil).

If you have fever and severe abdominal cramps, pass blood in your stools and generally feel like hell, you may have been unlucky enough to contract either amoebic or bacillary dysentery. If in doubt, see a doctor immediately and definitely see a physician once you return home because of possible long-term health effects.

- **Prickly Heat:** When you're in constant humidity, it's easy to develop a rash. Avoid it by powdering yourself in the morning and evening with talcum powder or powder containing zinc, such as Gold Bond. Also, avoid tight clothes.

- **Sun:** The sun is far more intense near the equator than anywhere else in the world. Gradual exposure to the sun--only 20-30 minutes recommended the first day, maximum--is mandatory to avoid that painful Larry-The-Lobster look. The sun is at its worst between ten and three. Wear sun block (SPF20 and higher) and drink lots of non-alcoholic liquid to keep from being dehydrated.

The sun probably will be the greatest danger you will encounter. Who wants to walk when their skin is the color of a Santa Claus suit and they're afraid it will crinkle with every step? It may be necessary to wear sunblock even on your lips. Be particularly careful to cover ears, jaws and the lower part of your neck. Also, sunglasses are essential. Bright sun reflected off the water is as much as 10,000 times brighter than is comfortable to the eye.

- **Sunstroke/Sun Poisoning:** OK, so you didn't listen. Symptoms of oncoming sunstroke are dizziness, vertigo, fevers, blister, headache, nausea, sudden lack of sweat and delusions. Get out of the heat immediately. Take a cool bath or shower. Drink fruit juices to replace lost electrolytes. If no improvement, see a doctor.

- **Fish Poisoning/Ciguatera:** A deadly toxin found primarily in reef fishes, such as snapper, very large grouper and barracuda. Symptoms include tingling, itching or numbness of the fingertips and lips, stomach cramps, nausea and vomiting. In severe cases, seek medical help immediately. It can be fatal. Freshness of the fish or its handling has nothing to do with whether the fish is tainted. It's a toxin that gets carried up the food chain; you get it from something you ate which also ate something which ate...

  Being at the top of the food chain, we may be the only ones who get sick from seafood. Fish don't seem to get ill from eating one another.

  Stick to ocean-roaming fish such as tuna, wahoo, mahimahi (dolphin fish, not Flipper) and you should have no problem. I once dined with eight people where we all ate from the same fish and one person got a mild case of ciguatera (lip tingling). Some scientists theorize it may also be a matter of individual susceptibility. Although it's been blamed for poisoning, fresh grouper is one of my favorite fish.

- **Finding a Doctor:** The likelihood of requiring medical attention is remote. To be prepared in case of an accident, know before you go: contact the International Association for Medical Assistance to Travelers, 745 5th Avenue, New York, NY 10022; or Intermedic, 777 3rd Avenue, New York 10017. They have the names and locations of well-trained English-speaking physicians all over the world. Remember to carry your insurance card if your policy covers overseas travel; otherwise, consider temporary medical/accident insurance.

Also, become a member of DAN, the Divers Alert Network, which transports members free of charge to the appropriate medical facility because of illness or accident, regardless of whether it's diving-related. It also offers $30,000 coverage of treatment expenses worldwide for any in-water diving or snorkeling accident. Most medical insurance does not pay for chamber treatment for the bends or an air embolism. For complete information, call toll free 800/446-2671.

## Jet Lag

The fatigue caused by jet lag can spoil the first few days of any long overseas trip that places you in a radically different time zone. Jet lag occurs because our bodies can't keep up with our speed of travel and instantly adopt to a new time schedule. It seems our bodies have their own inner clocks, called circadian rhythms, which are affected by the earth's rotation.

Some scientists claim that the biggest influence on our body rhythms is sunlight, therefore, we should spend as much time outdoors the first day as possible. If this theory is correct, we should always arrange for a daylight arrival at a new destination, since a nighttime arrival might actually prolong the effects of jet lag.

I like to stay awake at least until 7 p.m. on an eastbound trip, then take a sleeping pill that will assure me of 12 hours of uninterrupted sleep. That first long, tiring arrival day is reserved for relaxed sightseeing on land only.

I adopted this routine after becoming incredibly groggy on a dive in a place that was 16 hours ahead of my normal schedule. I'd never realized before that it was actually possible to fall asleep underwater!

# LARSEN ON BASS SERIES

(LB1) LARRY LARSEN ON BASS TACTICS is the ultimate "how-to" book that focuses on proven productive methods. It is dedicated to serious bass anglers - those who are truly interested in learning more about the sport and in catching more and larger bass each trip. Hundreds of highlighted tips and drawings explain how you can catch more and larger bass in waters all around the country. This reference source by America's best known bass fishing writer will be invaluable to both the avid novice and expert angler!

---

# BASS WATERS SERIES
## by Larry Larsen

Take the guessing game out of your next bass fishing trip. The most productive bass waters in each Florida region are described in this multi-volume series, including boat ramps, seasonal tactics, water characteristics and much more. Both popular and overlooked locations are detailed with numerous maps and photos. The author has lived and fished extensively in each region of the state over the past 25 years.

(BW1) GUIDE TO NORTH FLORIDA BASS WATERS - Covers from Orange Lake north and west. Includes Lakes Orange, Lochloosa, Talquin and Seminole, the St. Johns, Nassau, Suwannee and Apalachicola Rivers and many more of the region's best! You'll learn where bass bite in Keystone Lakes, Newnans Lake, St. Mary's River, Doctors Lake, Black Creek, Juniper Lake, Ortega River, Lake Jackson, Lake Miccosukee, Chipola River, Deer Point Lake, Blackwater River, Panhandle Mill Ponds and many more!

(BW2) GUIDE TO CENTRAL FLORIDA BASS WATERS - Covers from Tampa/Orlando to Palatka. Includes Lakes George, Rodman, Monroe, Tarpon and the Harris Chain, the St. Johns, Oklawaha and Withlacoochee Rivers and many others! You'll find the best spots to fish in the Ocala Forest, Crystal River, Hillsborough River, Conway Chain, Homosassa River, Lake Minneola, Lake Weir, Lake Hart, Spring Runs and many more!

(BW3) GUIDE TO SOUTH FLORIDA BASS WATERS - Covers from I-4 to the Everglades. Includes Lakes Tohopekaliga, Kissimmee, Okeechobee, Poinsett, Tenoroc and Blue Cypress, the Winter Haven Chain and many more! You'll learn where bass can be caught in Fellsmere Farm 13. Caloosahatchee River, Lake June-in-Winter, Lake Hatchineha, the Everglades, Lake Istokpoga, Peace River, Crooked Lake, Lake Osborne, St. Lucie Canal, lake Trafford, Shell Creek, Lake Marian, Myakka River, Lake Pierce, Webb Lake and many more!

> For more than 20 years, award-winning author Larry Larsen has studied and written about bass fishing. His angling adventures are extensive, from Canada to Honduras and from Cuba to Hawaii. He is Florida Editor for *Outdoor Life* and contributor to all major outdoor magazines.

# OUTDOOR TRAVEL SERIES

## by Larry Larsen and M. Timothy O'Keefe

Candid guides with inside information on the best charters, time of the year, and other important recommendations that can make your next fishing and/or diving trip much more enjoyable.

(OT1) FISH & DIVE THE CARIBBEAN - Vol. 1 Northern Caribbean, including Cozumel, Cayman Islands, The Bahamas, Jamaica, Virgin Islands and other popular destinations. Required reading for fishing and diving enthusiasts who want to know the most cost-effective means to enjoy these Caribbean islands. You'll learn how to select the best destination and plan appropriately for your specific interests.

(OT3) FISH & DIVE FLORIDA & The Keys - Includes in-depth information on where and how to plan a vacation to America's most popular fishing and diving destination. Special features include artificial reef loran numbers; freshwater springs/caves; coral reefs/barrier islands; gulf stream/passes; inshore flats/channels; and back country estuaries.

(OT2) FISH & DIVE THE CARIBBEAN - Vol. 2 - *COMING SOON!* Southern Caribbean, including Guadeloupe, Costa Rica, Venezuela, other destinations.

---

"Fish & Dive the Caribbean, Vol. 1" was one of four finalists in the Best Book Content Category of the National Association of Independent Publishers 1991 competition. Over 500 books were submitted by various U.S. publishers, including Simon & Schuster and Turner Publishing, Inc. Said the NAIP judges "An excellent source book with invaluable instructions for fishing or diving. Written by two nationally-known experts who, indeed, know what vacationing can be!"

---

# DIVING SERIES

## by M. Timothy O'Keefe

(DL1) DIVING TO ADVENTURE will inform and entertain novice and experienced divers alike with its in-depth discussion of how to get the most enjoyment from diving and snorkeling. Aimed at divers around the country, the book shows how to get started in underwater photography, how to use current to your advantage, how to avoid seasickness, how to dive safely after dark, and more. Special sections detail how to plan a dive vacation, including live-aboard diving.

---

M. Timothy O'Keefe was editor of the first major dive travel guidebook published in the U.S. The award-winning author writes for numerous diving, travel and sportfishing publications.

# COASTAL FISHING GUIDES

(FG1) FRANK SARGEANT'S SECRET SPOTS - Tampa Bay to Cedar Key - A unique "where-to" book of detailed secret spots for Florida's finest saltwater fishing. This guide book describes little-known honeyholes and tells exactly how to fish them. Prime seasons, baits and lures, marinas and dozens of detailed maps of the prime spots are included. A comprehensive index helps the reader to further pinpoint productive areas and tactics.

( FG2) FRANK SARGEANT'S SECRET SPOTS -Southwest Florida
*COMING SOON!!*

# INSHORE SERIES

## by Frank Sargeant

(IL1) THE SNOOK BOOK-"Must" reading for anyone who loves the pursuit of this unique sub-tropic species. Every aspect of how you can find and catch big snook is covered, in all seasons and all waters where snook are found.

(IL2) THE REDFISH BOOK-Packed with expertise from the nation's leading redfish anglers and guides, this book covers every aspect of finding and fooling giant reds. You'll learn secret techniques revealed for the first time. After reading this informative book, you'll catch more redfish on your next trip!

(IL3) THE TARPON BOOK-Find and catch the wily "silver king" along the Gulf Coast, north through the mid-Atlantic, and south along Central and South American coastlines. Numerous experts share their most productive techniques.

(IL4) THE TROUT BOOK -Jammed with tips from the nation's leading trout guides and light tackle anglers. For both the old salt and the rank amateur who pursue the spotted weakfish, or seatrout, throughout the coastal waters of the Gulf and Atlantic.

Frank Sargeant is a renown outdoor writer and expert on saltwater angler. He has traveled throughout the state and Central America in pursuit of all major inshore species. Sargeant is Outdoor Editor of the Tampa Tribune and a Senior Writer for *Southern Saltwater* and *Southern Outdoors* magazines.

# HUNTING LIBRARY

## by John E. Phillips

**(DH1) MASTERS' SECRETS OF DEER HUNTING** - Increase your deer hunting success significantly by learning from the masters of the sport. New information on tactics and strategies for bagging deer is included in this book, the most comprehensive of its kind.

**(DH2) THE SCIENCE OF DEER HUNTING** - Covers why, where and when a deer moves and deer behavior. Find the answers to many of the toughest deer hunting problems a sportsman ever encounters!

**(TH1) MASTERS' SECRETS OF TURKEY HUNTING** - Masters of the sport have solved some of the most difficult problems you will encounter while hunting wily longbeards with bows, blackpowder guns and shotguns. Learn the 10 deadly sins of turkey hunting and what to do if you commit them.

# FISHING LIBRARY

**(CF1) MASTERS' SECRETS OF CRAPPIE FISHING** by John E. Phillips - Learn how to make crappie start biting again once they have stopped, how to select the color of jig to catch the most and biggest crappie, how to find crappie when a cold front hits and how to catch them in 100-degree heat as well as through the ice. Unusual but productive crappie fishing techniques are included. Whether you are a beginner or a seasoned crappie fisherman, this book will improve your catch!

# OUTDOOR ADVENTURE LIBRARY

## by Vin T. Sparano, Editor-in-Chief, Outdoor Life

**(OA1) HUNTING DANGEROUS GAME** -It's a special challenge to hunt dangerous game - those dangerous animals that hunt back! Live the adventure of tracking a rogue elephant, surviving a grizzly attack, facing a charging Cape buffalo and driving an arrow into a giant brown bear at 20 feet. These classic tales will make you very nervous next time you're in the woods!

**(OA2) GAME BIRDS & GUN DOGS** - A unique collection of stories about hunters, their dogs and the upland game and waterfowl they hunt. These tales are about those remarkable shots and unexplainable misses. You will read about good gun dogs and heart-breaking dogs, but never about bad dogs, because there's no such animal.

# INDEX

## A

acupressure wristbands  89
advanced travel  125
Adventure Express  140
Aegean  138
artifacts  43-50
artificial light  40
artificial reefs  61
audiologist  91
Australia  14, 124

## B

baking soda  144
barracuda  16
basket starfish  54
bicycling  75
Big Pine Key  122
bike race  75
Bonaire  3, 117, 118, 127
Bonine  88
bully net  64

## C

California  123
camcorder  34
Cancun  121
Cayman Islands  120
Charlotte Amalie  118
cleaner-shrimp  52
"clearing ears"  93
close-up lens  39
cola beverages  88
colds  96, 145
compact cameras  31
conductive hearing loss  93
corals  17, 18, 52, 144
cortisone cream  144
costs of travel  100
Cousteau, Jacques  4, 10, 13
Cozumel  120
Crystal River  130, 139
current  67-74, 121

cyalumes  73

## D

deceptive advertising  115
dehydration  145
Delos, Greece  137, 140
diarrhea  146
Divers Alert Network  148
dramamine  88
drift diving  67

## E

equipment  104

## F

Fiji  135
film  105
finding a doctor  147
first aid kit  58, 104
"Fish & Dive Florida & The
     Keys."  118
"Fish & Dive the Caribbean"  118
fixate  88, 89
float line  73
Florida Keys  122, 123
foul weather  110
fraud  115
Freeman, Douglas S.  4

## G

George Town  120
ginger  88
gloves  56
Grand Cayman  120, 134
Great Barrier Reef  124
Greece  137
grouper  16
Guam  137
Gulf of Aqaba, Red Sea  134, 139

# H

habituation 87
hand signals 57
Hass, Dr. Hans 4, 15
hearing aids 91, 94
Heron Island, Australia 124, 132, 139
humidity 145

# I

Ikelite Underwater Systems 28
insurance 104
International Association for Medical Assistance 147
intestinal problems 146
"island time" 141

# J

jet lag 148
John Pennekamp Coral Reef State Park 122

# K

Key Largo 122
Key West 122

# L

La Paz, Mexico 138, 140
lemon 88
liability release 111
live-aboard diving 107-116
lobster 59-66
Looe Key 122
Los Islotes 138
Los Padres National Forest 124

# M

macro-photography 37-42
Madang, Papua, New Guinea 136, 140
Magen's Bay 118
"mal de mer" 86
manatees 130, 139

Manta Ray Bay Hotel 140
mantas 137
Marathon 122
Matagi 135
medical attention 147
Mexico 138
Micronesia 126, 137
Middle Keys 122
Molasses Reef 122
moray eel 59, 62
mosquitoes 144
motion sickness 86
Mullin, Dr. Tom 91

# N

National Geographic Magazine 118
natural insect repellents 145
New Guinea 126
night diving 51-58, 73
Nikon School of Underwater Photography 36
Nikonos 36, 40
no-see-ums 144
North Channel Islands 124
North Shore, Providenciales 130
North Wall 120
nudibranchs 20

# O

odors 89
otolaryngologist 95
oxidation 48

# P

P&O Resort Holidays 125
P&O Resorts, Ltd. 139
package deals 100
Palau 137
Papaya 144
perforated ear drum 92
peripheral vestibular mechanism 86
photography 67, 98
Poseidon Ventures Dive Tours 126
potassium 145
prickly heat 146

Provo, Turks & Caicos 139

Q

Qamea, Fiji 135, 139

R

Red Sea 134
repellent 144
Research Submersible Ltd. 120
Roessler, Carl 111

S

safety divers 77
salt supplements 145
San Juan 119
sand flies 144
Santa Barbara 124
scorpionfish 55, 57, 62
scuba vacations 117-127
sea anemones 52
sea horse 21-26
sea legs 87
sea lions 138
Sea Safaris 127, 139, 140
sea urchins 16, 54, 62
seasickness 85-90
See & Sea 111
Seychelles 127
sharks 14-16
shipwrecks 45, 98
shore diving 99
shrimp 20
sight-seeing 67
sinus condition 96
skill levels 98
"Skin So Soft" 144
small claims court 113
snorkeling 129-138
Solomon, Charles 86
South Seas 136
souvenir hunting 43
spearfishing 67, 98
spiny lobster 60, 61
sponges 19
St. Thomas 118

Stewart, Don 3
Sting Ray City, Grand Cayman 132, 139
sun 146
"swimmers ear" 92

T

taxes and tips 100
"tickling" 63
Travel Seychelles 127
trip cancellation insurance 116
Tropical Adventures 140, 141
Truk 126
Truk Continental 126
trunkfish 55
Truth Aquatics Inc 124
Tulum 121
Turks & Caicos 131

U

U.S. Customs 104
U.S. Virgin Islands 119
"Undercurrent" 113
underwater housings
  EWA-Marine 28
  Ikelite Underwater Systems 28
  Motor Marine II 30
  Nikonos 29
underwater photography 27-35

V

vacations 97-105
vertigo 58, 86
video cameras 32

Y

Yap, Micronesia 137, 140

Breinigsville, PA USA
25 June 2010
240552BV00004B/8/P